UNRECONSTRUCTED

T0069083

UNRECONSTRUCTED

POEMS SELECTED AND NEW

Ed Ochester

Autumn House Press

PITTSBURGH

"Autumn House" and "Autumn House Press" are registered trademarks owned by Autumn House Press, a non-profit corporation whose mission is the publication and promotion of poetry and other fine literature.

Autumn House Press Staff
Executive Director: Richard St. John
Executive Editor and Founder: Michael Simms
Community Outreach Director: Michael Wurster
Co-Director: Eva-Maria Simms
Special Projects Coordinator: Joshua Storey
Associate Editor: Anna Catone
Associate Editor: Laurie Mansell Reich
Consulting Editor: Ziggy Edwards
Media Consultant: Jan Beatty
Tech Crew Chief: Michael Milberger

ISBN 978-1-932870-14-5
Library of Congress Control Number 2007920911

All Autumn House books are printed on acid-free paper and meet the international standards of permanent books intended for purchase by libraries.

BOOKS BY ED OCHESTER

Unreconstructed: Poems Selected and New
American Poetry Now: Pitt Poetry Series (editor)
The Land of Cockaigne
Snow White Horses: Selected Poems, 1973-1988
The Pittsburgh Book of Contemporary American Poetry (co-editor)
Changing the Name to Ochester
Miracle Mile
Dancing on the Edges of Knives

Limited Editions

The Republic of Lies
Cooking in Key West
Allegheny
Weehawken Ferry
A Drift of Swine
Natives (editor)
The Third Express
The Great Bourgeois Bus Company
We Like It Here

THE AUTUMN HOUSE POETRY SERIES

• Winner of the annual Autumn House Poetry Prize

CONTENTS

ACKNOWLEDGMENTS

Thanks to the editors of the following publications, where some of the "New Poems" first appeared:

Agni: Butterfly Effect, The Origin of Myth
Alaska Review: September, Listening to the Old Songs
American Poetry Review: Fred Astaire, Sage, Writers' Colony
Barrow Street: Rewinding the Cassette of Fear City,
    Voltaire at Cirey, 1736
Café Review: The Fireplace
Green Mountains Review: Grouchos
Nightsun: March of the Penguins
One Trick Pony: Poem Written in the Manner of David Lehman
Ploughshares: Pasta
Poetry International: What I Learned from the Roseanne Show
Prairie Schooner: Unreconstructed

"Pasta" was selected for *Best American Poems, 2007* by Heather McHugh.

Thanks to Story Line Press for permission to reprint poems from *The Land of Cockaigne*.

Thanks to Britt and Ned and Betsy for their enduring love and help and patience.

Thanks to the Pittsburgh gang, in particular Jan Beatty, Lynn Emanuel, Lori Jakiela, Chuck Kinder, Dave Newman, Mike Simms, Gerry Stern, and my long-term friend and colleague Judy Vollmer.

Thanks to the Bennington people: my students, who have made the pedagogical life worth living; Cilla, Victoria, and Elaine, for their sweetness and enthusiasm; Virgil Suarez, for cigars, parties, and soul; and, not least, Liam Rector, with whom I have argued and celebrated for more than 20 years.

Thanks to Yaddo and the MacDowell Colony for residencies restorative and productive, and to Gary Metras of Adastra Press for his terrific letterpress work.

NEW POEMS

THE ORIGIN OF MYTH

That summer I was drinking
apple cider vinegar because I read
in an obscure book it was good
for my health. A tablespoon or two
in a glass of spring water, with a bit
of honey or raw sugar. Controls weight,
the book said, flushes harmful toxins
from joints, tissues and organs.
"Doctor George Blodgett drank it
every day, and remained vigorous
until his death at age 94."
                                        One reads
and perhaps believes almost anything
when one has lived alone for a while.
I felt good, doing it, though perhaps
that was because I walked on the beach
every day, swam, then walked again,
collected beach glass smoothed by the waves.
Pale blue and green, like solidified air,
dark green like emeralds, very rarely
sapphire blue and once a tiny piece
of red round as the pupil of an eye.
No one was on the beach because it was
September, and I had a white cabin
to myself. I swam and walked and read
and ate sparingly. I had come there
to be alone, and to think things through.
Every morning I drank my vinegar.
I read that the soldier who gave Jesus
vinegar on a sponge did so not in mockery
but in pity, to offer a restorative.
After a week I set the "red eye" on my desk

so we could watch one another. At dusk
the mist far out over the water looked like
distant hills, and I understood how
an earlier inhabitant might have thought
these were mountains that rose at nightfall
and disappeared with the dawn.

THE FIREPLACE

How skillful I am with fire,
not that it takes much:
open the flue when you start it
for maximum combustion, then
close it for maximum heat.
You need sticks & seasoned logs
and of course dry kindling, so
I'm wadding up newspapers with photos
of George W. Bush and Jennifer Lopez,
the semi-comatose Pope and ads for bad movies,
a letter from someone I no longer trust.
What more could one want? Heat and
purification, something to watch
with a glass of wine before bed
as snow continues to fall.

I prefer sunshine, of course, and
woods with warblers singing, streams filled
with trout and pure water, but this
has something to say for it, comfort
in my isolation, and all the nonsense
and evil, the gossip of this world,
the tongues of snakes,
ashes, ashes, ashes.

REWINDING THE CASSETTE OF FEAR CITY

Before Melanie Griffith gets a breast
enhancement and a voice coach   before
Tom Berenger confronts his violent past
as a boxer—as we all must confront our pasts,
that tedious duty   before the mad killer who
has vowed to extinguish "the worthless lives"
of strippers and junkies   before Rae Dawn Chong
gets slashed   before Billy Dee Williams proclaims
the sanctity of Law as he administers an illegal
beating to a handcuffed Tom Berenger   before
Vittorio Brazo—the Don—eats his elegant *melanzana*
in a Little Italy which in the real world
has disappeared   before the shots of Times Square
before it was sold to Disney—Times Square as
electric Eden festooned with neon jellybeans,
"anything is possible"   and to the credits where
it clicks.   Jerks to a stop

and we're ready to begin again
the essential American story:
the titanic battle between the forces
of psychopathic puritanism and
the fun of inevitable sleaze

VOLTAIRE AT CIREY, 1736

Emilie, the love of his life,
took him to her castle
where they built laboratories
and libraries and workrooms
for the life of the mind
as well as the bed
and studied Newton
and Locke and recruited neighbors
to act in plays and read poetry
aloud at 4 a.m. and enjoyed
"exquisite food and wine"
and such were the times
that even Emilie's husband
became fond of Voltaire
and once, catching the great man
with another woman, scolded him
for being "unfaithful to us."

Perhaps this is what the phrase
"the Enlightenment" means,
though their behavior titillated
most of France which acted like us
reading *People* and *Star*
clucking, sanctimonious and jealous—
slaves to our sadnesses, envious—
though of course we'd draw a blank
at the Newton and the Locke
and the poetry parts.

WRITERS' COLONY

—for Starkey Flythe

How contrary it is
the human heart, how
it's propelled by opposites.
A friend of mine said years ago
"a really good poem sure
gets the snot flowing" and
for anyone who *has* a heart anymore
that says almost as much about *it*
as Frost or Pound ever said;
and at breakfast this morning
when we were joking about Nancy Reagan's
imaginary stay at Yaddo, writing *My Turn*,
how she was responsible for the best
elements of the décor ("Really?"
said Mark, coming in late)
why did we laugh? What a strange
mixture of malice, pain and the absurd!
Not that I've ever been down too long myself,
you understand, though some of whatever
are "my best" poems have come from
the long night around us and, for example,
after the ice storm yesterday, this morning
we're chattering like sparrows
about the bright sun on the snow.

FRED ASTAIRE

The secret of his popularity was
that he looked like a bus driver
who could dance. In my teens
I hated his movies, and told my Aunt Carrie
they were corny and "unrealistic"
but she just laughed and said "you go
to his movies because they *ain't* realistic,"
Aunt Carrie who worked as a file clerk
and spent an hour each way on the subway
commuting. And later, if I'd been honest,
I would have realized that's why I loved
Dickens and Keats, his "Grecian Urn," and
doesn't Fred look a bit like Carlos Williams
who also talks plain without ornament just
like Astaire when he's singing? A critic said
he had "an unspectacular voice" and lacked
"the vocal technique of a trained singer" but
had great respect for the lyrics and "immaculate
timing," so that even Mel Torme called him,
as a jazz singer, "the greatest bar none,"
and how wonderful that the man who danced
with Ginger Rogers and Rita Hayworth and Judy
Garland and worked with the Gershwins,
Ira and George, and Noel Coward
was "really" named Frederick Austerlitz,
the son of an immigrant, and that when he took
his first screen test some moron—probably
an early critic of Williams, too—reported to his boss:
"can't act, can't sing, balding, can dance
a little."
       No wonder Carrie loved him
as she shuttled underground in New York

where nearly everyone if they worked
their asses off 40-plus a week got "enough
to live on" and, like most Americans,
lived on dreams.

THE REPUBLIC OF LIES

Henriette von Schirach, wife
of the Nazi Youth leader,
one night in Amsterdam saw
S.S. troops rounding up
Jewish women and girls
for transport to the camps.
She was shocked.
Can you imagine that?
And what could Baldur,
her American husband
tell her? Finally
at the Berghof
in the presence of Himmler
and Borman she blurted it
to Hitler: "why do we have
to kill women and girls?"

Hitler could be generous
to friends. He was
furious, but did nothing
other than distrust Baldur
from then on.
Imagine talking
to power that way
for the deaths
of a few nameless
women and girls.

What good would it do?
What was she thinking?

UNRECONSTRUCTED

When people talk about Form
distrust them.
These are the ones
who believe the starving
have themselves to blame
but that the sonnet
has a life of its own.
They believe in eagles,
two-headed kinds and
the ones they've hunted
near to extinction.
They're headed for
a retirement villa
in the sky and don't
really want your kind
there, just as they didn't
want your kind here.
They believe human nature
never changes (and don't
like ancient history either
since it's about different
human natures). Remember when
you were happiest? Remember
when you were first truly
sexually happy
(if you ever were)?
They say that's
just a pale reflection
of what's Real, they say
prepare yourself for death.

BUTTERFLY EFFECT

Forgive me, friend, because
I am thinking of a particular
sad Buddhist who has no
real friends anymore and
worries about his alcoholism and
is convinced that he desires nothing, and
I'm thinking of my old friend Walter
who talks to Jesus now and lectures
on creationism because he hasn't
held a job for twenty years and
whose wife died young of cancer
and who knows that he is "saved," and
I'm thinking of all the Americans
who believe that in former lives
they were Catherine the Great or Nefertiti,
and all the ones who believe
in the butterfly effect, e.g.:
some jerk who farts in Albuquerque
might trigger a typhoon in Sumatra,
though if that were true
we'd have more storms than Jupiter and
the earth already would be destroyed—
maybe the fluttering butterflies and the farts
cancel one another out, except for
particularly strong ones—and
I am thinking: "the greatest
country in the world since Rome" and
all us poor dumb fucks
heads filled with shit
muttering to ourselves
as we plod along.

BLACK ICE

At approximately 10:00 pm
my old Nissan Pathfinder begins
to fishtail on 380 and spins
180 degrees and over the berm
into a bank where it rides up
and then finally
overturns

                   and I discover
myself upside down suspended
by belts as the cassette of Mozart's
Piano Concerto #13 doesn't miss a beat
(Mitsuko Uchida's terrific!
tangles of silver) and
the motor's still running—
broken gas line! gigantic
fireballs!—as the flashers
blink and the elegant music
swells and flourishes as
I thrash around in the belts and
try to open the crushed door
as in the rearview a small red
pulse appears and slowly
enlarges

THANK YOU

My friend Rosina has a toast:
"for wealth and for health but not for love"
which translates into and out of Spanish as
"fuck you," which reminds me of
David Lehman's brilliant poem in which
he discovers that "thank you"
often means "fuck you" but that
"fuck you" never means "thank you"
though I would wish to extend
this insight to the international sphere
where, say, the ambassador from
the United States says: "I would like
to commend the ambassador of France
for his most constructive comments
on the Middle East situation.
Thank you." Or the ambassador
from Syria says "We thank
the ambassador of the United States
for his thoughts on the orderly supply
of oil to the major industrialized nations."
And then of course there is the president
of the corporation who as he presents
the gold watch says "for fifty years
of loyal and faithful service we
want to say 'Thank You'"—and those nights
at the Oscars when the winners for
sound production and best boy and gaffer
stand up and endlessly say "thank you
thank you thank you"—and the professor
who says to his graduate student

"for your corrections of fact to my essay
'Manifestations of Camp Sensibility in *Paradise Lost,
Book One*' I can only say 'thank you'
but you will find that in the future
I will never forget
your contribution."

POEM WRITTEN IN THE MANNER
OF DAVID LEHMAN

Thanks to the snowstorm which
has stranded us at the KGB Bar
I am able to hear you paraphrase
your lecture on the construction
of the 59th Street Bridge and
your entertaining theory that
in the Simon & Garfunkel song
of the same name "feeling groovy"
refers to the sensation of driving
their VW Beetle over the ruts
worn into its asphalt in the 60's
the decade when mafia boss
Sam Giancana almost put out
a hit order on Frank Sinatra
who does my favorite version
of "Dancing in the Dark" (the song)
which like sex with a famous poet
offers greater pleasure than that felt
by an inmate of Cleveland
experiencing Monet's "Water Lilies"
for the first time at MOMA
let go of my hand please
but I can also tell you
about the winter night at the 5 SPOT
when Ornette Coleman
squealed "My Favorite Things"
through his tiny plastic sax
at me and Kenneth and Ed
as we leaned against the john door

and then everyone and I
took the "A" train
back to Columbia (the university)
where I had just received a letter
from the soon-to-be-famous
Jacques Derrida.

MARCH OF THE PENGUINS

"The editor of National Review urged [Young Republicans] to see the movie because it promoted monogamy. A widely circulated Christian magazine said it made 'a strong case for intelligent design'" —*The New York Times,* 9/13/05

What the hell are they going to do now
with the libidinous bluebird, who lines up
a couple of extra girlfriends every summer,
not to mention the evil house wrens—
don't be fooled by their cheery little calls,
they have up to five mates at a time!
I won't even mention the gay rabbits
we had once, in love with one another's ears,
etc., and even now my old friend Walter may be
declaiming how God planted dinosaur bones
to test the faith of Christians with the *appearance*
of evolution, thereby demonstrating once again
we are the first country to pass from barbarism
to decadence without an interlude, and as for
"intelligent design," even Britney Spears
wouldn't drop her eggs
at 70 below.

IRONIES OF HISTORY

—for Judith Vollmer

Napoleon's father sued his upstairs neighbor
for emptying a chamberpot on his head so that—
Corsicans carried on feuds forever!—
years later the neighbor's son persuaded
the Emperor of Russia to hate Napoleon and
since you're going to the American Academy in Rome
and always wondered why a Polish ancestor
of yours lived in Italy I should tell you that
Prince Eugene, Napoleon's Viceroy in Italy,
recruited Polish troops for his army which
in the Russian campaign was nearly annihilated
at the river Wop, west of Smolensk, which
doesn't seem so much "ironic" as absurd, as does
the fact that when Napoleon was working
one day at Mombello he heard noises behind a screen
and discovered his sister Pauline screwing
one of his staff officers, a man one historian
calls "small, slight and colourless," who
after marrying Pauline aped his brother-in-law
by walking up and down with his hat sideways
and his hands behind his back but luckily
he died of yellow fever in Haiti so that Napoleon
could marry her off to Prince Camillo Borghese,
wealthiest man in Italy, one of whose many titles
was Baron Crapolatri.

WHY I LOVE TEENAGERS

In Holiday Park, PA
the Burger King
has put out a signboard
advertising
for late-night employees
and some kid
contemptuous
of minimum wage
or the "free enterprise" system
and possibly even
"In God We Trust"
has stolen the "C" from the sign
so that it reads:
"NOW HIRING   LOSERS"

THEODICY

In New Orleans
God punished:
fornicators and fornicatrixes, or
George W. Bush, or
the tribe of Ham, or
the tribe of Benjamin, or
Alzheimerites, or
the unemployed, or
white landlords, or
Paul Prudhomme, or
cats, dogs and canaries, or
levees, or
the secret juju gods of
        the Louis Armstrong Airport, or
brass musical instruments, or
Ms. Marcella D. Washington, or
zydeco, or
pride, sloth, greed, gluttony, lust,
        anger and envy, or
Cokie Roberts, or
Snowball the dog, or
the Tulane Green Wave, or
the Bourbon Street Tabernacle Choir, or
Catholics with 8 plus children, or
Catholics with no children, or
evangelicals in wheelchairs, or
pro-life activists, or
children and fetuses, or
none of the above, or
all of the above

WHAT I LEARNED FROM THE ROSEANNE SHOW

I like Roseanne,
she sounds like a duck,
and as I watch her this morning
with my mother who is 92 and
dozing off in the heat and
who is largely deaf anyway and
who leaves on the tv because
these mysterious images are
a window onto a world she
resigned from years ago,
I perceive that Roseanne
is at a monster car rally
and drag strip and is talking
to a black woman kickboxer who
brags that she can "beat the [bleep]
out of any man" and proceeds
to demonstrate her skills against
two men out of whom she beats
the [bleep] & then Roseanne interviews
a gorgeous Asian stunt woman and
kickboxer in a black leotard who
demonstrates with the same two guys
that she also can kick the [bleep]
out of any man, and then Roseanne
gets into a monster truck with
tires the size of small houses
and flattens a couple of junker cars
and at this point Mom wakes up and shouts
"WHAT ARE THEY DOING?" and I shout

"ROSEANNE IS TEACHING YOUNG WOMEN
TO BE AS VIOLENT AS ANY TEENAGE
BOY JERK" and Mom laughs and
shouts "THAT ROSEANNE!" and shuffles
into the kitchen where two hours
before lunchtime she takes out
the tuna salad so it won't be
too cold for her teeth.

PASTA

In college I loved Browning's phrase—
was it in "Two in the Campagna"?—
"tangled ropes of lasagna" and even today
I think it may have been pasta which
civilized the Italians so much they
refused to fight for Mussolini—remember how
Marshall Badoglio's armies surrendered in Africa
tutti and *rapidamente*?—and even the names
make you smile: orecchiette ("little lambs ears")
and orzo and penne and rigatoni and
of course gay bow-tie farfalle which
make me think of my favorite restaurant,
Flavio's, where the fat cook pounds his evil veal
but Nuncia is still beautiful and smiles as
she serves prawns and home-made fettuccine,
yes, and even surly Mencken called Puccini's music
"silver macaroni, exquisitely tangled"
and how lovely is "angel hair,"
semolina spun into a mist of pasta
that needs only some oil of the olive
and a few peppers or spring peas
to transport you to heaven and
whose preparation teaches
a great truth about cooking
and pleasure: focus, don't overdo it:
al dente, al dente.

GROUCHOS

On the beach at Popp's Motel in Key Largo
an enormous family—kids to grandpas—
floats face down in snorkel gear
in one foot of water over a sandy bottom
utterly devoid of coral or fish—"Look Tommy"
a daddy shouts, "that weed looks like a starfish," and
then three more of them—one with a Groucho moustache—
walk into the shallows with fly rods
that have bobbers on the ends and
snorkel a hundred yards down the beach holding
rods in the air with one hand while they propel
themselves with enormous flippers and
stand up to fish in water a foot deep,
and now two more of them come out of their room
with rods and flippers, walking
in a keep-on-truckin' motion, and
next to me a kid about six starts to repeat
his catechism to his mom who's lying in a hammock
and he says "Jesus hung on the cross for me so I'll get
to go to heaven, but Jason *won't* go to heaven,
right?" and his mommy says "that's right"
and I'm thinking they should really all
be wearing Groucho glasses and moustaches, but
gentle reader, before you decide that
I'm just one more poetry snob
and take umbrage at the fact—though why not
take umbrage, it's free?—let me emphasize:

I myself am staying at Popp's Motel
and though perhaps it's too much to say that
"I love" these people, this is after all
my native land and I too participate

in what Herbert Muller called "the highest
standard of low living in the world,"
and even my own father, back from his first trip
to Florida years ago, told about a guy killed
by a falling coconut (food was free,
but sometimes dangerous!) and marveled
how oranges cost next to nothing and how
a man could live on the earlybird specials
like a king for almost nothing, so that
half my family with their bobbing heads
flew down here to live foreverafter in
large pink lonely houses by canals
and watch reruns by the sea—

                    and now
a grandpa Groucho with a gut bigger than
Minnesota Fats' walks out to the dock and
throws *his* line with bobber into a foot of water
and yells to his wife "THROW ME THE GODDAM
BLUE MESH BAG" and where not even a minnow
is visible casts and casts again,
"GIVE IT TO ME, GIVE IT TO ME
THE BLUE MESH BAG,
JESUS H. CHRIST"

SAGE

—for Mary Morse

Mary attends a zen center
in Westchester where the zenbo
is the father of Uma Thurman
and no doubt a comfort
to his client stockbrokers
and copywriters plus a good story
to chat about as they drive home
to Tarrytown past the IBM building

though it's all at a great remove
from my garden lost among
the failed farms of Pennsylvania
where I'm weeding and pruning
and accidentally disrupt a log
and watch a thousand ants pour out
ready to protect the queen

so helpless they remind me
of James Wright's poem in which
he refers to a saint who refuses
to enter nirvana because
"his scruffy dog, suppurating at the nostrils
and half mad with rabies, could not
accompany him into perfect peace"

though I've never felt that way
about dogs, which come and go,
just as we come and go, but I want
to prune this sage bush,
dead twigs among gray leaves
textured like lizard skin,
to make it perfect
before it goes

SEPTEMBER, LISTENING TO THE OLD SONGS

—for Terrance Hayes

When I'm feeling sad I play old stuff
and so tonight, some Creem and
Neil's *Trans*, and Van's "Into the Mystic,"
a little Dead, and then I go into the dark
under the trees and think I see a trace of
the northern lights, maybe not, but the stars
are enormous and after the music a great stillness
and so dark I imagine that sitting
on a bench I am in a small
boat in the middle of the sea, so alone
that I forget I am alone, except
for a few crickets, and they remind me
of what Terrance said to a friend
leaving for a Zen monastery out west—
anything older than that?—he said
"I hope you find nothing," which was
perfect, and here under the stars
once again I realize it is perfect
as, after most sadness,
it always is.

DANCING ON THE EDGES OF KNIVES

ON A FRIEND WHOSE WORK HAS COME TO NOTHING

At school you dove off the bridge at night
in a swan, down to the half-dozen girls
treading water to keep up with you.
Then, cock of the walk, you'd strut off
with some chick while the rest of us
were left to drink lukewarm beer and cluck.

Those were the Dylan Thomas days when
wearing baggy tweeds you picked up west of Wales
you told *Under Milk Wood* so that all the dead below
were wet with tears. Then
you'd cut out with a casual girl
and leave us to dismantle the scene.

Those were also the Norman Mailer days,
the quiet admonitions to suck the smoke in deep,
the blue morning jogs around the lake.
You were the last descendant of the Grand Duke
  Maximilian,
and every one of us was the true illegitimate
son of Hemingway who
by the way
was your very close friend.

You made yourself the prince of days
because you cracked imagination's cipher,
taught us to ignore the telegrams
from the past that never came,
found at the heart of our onion
the nothing you'd been sure was there.
So. Our banquets and pioneer characters
were spun from brightness in the air.

Christ, while we thought each thud of our typewriters
was tough enough to puncture hearts
you heard America snapping its gum
and laughed and fluted tunes
through the public forests
on the coast of pacific despair.

Thus, seeing a one-inch notice of your death
in a small-town Midwest paper,
it is difficult to say exactly
what death has taken in.
A politician among the apes,
a hummingbird above the snails.

But the rest of us—
Lord, vaguely amazed at your death,
corrupt as you but less successful,
still losing twenty dreams a year
like irreplaceable feathers—
the rest of us at least 2000 miles
behind you are still crawling outward
toward our mythical west coast.

WHEN THE DOW JONES INDUSTRIAL INDEX
HIT ITS ALL-TIME HIGH IN 1966

Just then children began to disappear,
just then blood began to accumulate in the lowlands,
springs of blood resumed their flow
in Kansas and Mississippi,
blood pooled
in Chicago, Dallas, Los Angeles.
Just then supertankers of blood
began to arrive from Asia
to pump their cargo
into the harbors and streets of the cities.
And even in the small cities
and on the failing farms
men slept at night
like caged wolves,
smelling blood in their dreams,
tiny bubbles of blood
welling up in their nostrils.

AFTER ADVERTISING ENDED

small children starved to death,
mothers did not know how to lactate
and wore brassieres over their eyes,
telephone wire was cut into belts and ties,
airplanes were worshiped
and cars lathered with acne lotion;
thousands of women migrated into the Atlantic, singing,
and bewildered young lovers
tentatively put their thumbs in their ears.

REPORTER, AUGUST OF '62

I'm sitting in the precinct house
in Far Rockaway. The detective sergeant
flips through a *Playboy*, stops at the centerfold.
"Tellya how bad it is kid,
they piss out the winders whenya walk downa street.
Even the jews startin amove."
Here's lookin at you, kid.

I'd like to see those pictures in his drawer.

Two cops bring in a black kid & throw him in the cage.
No shirt. Blood on his shoulder.
Smiling in shock. Or smiling. "Cocksuckers."
The cops move toward him. The wound
with its tiny puckered lips, the blood
the rose of great peace.

THE PENN CENTRAL STATION AT BEACON, N.Y.

An immense room as quiet
as an elephant graveyard
without spines or tusks.
Dust in the slantlight from windows
twenty feet up the wall.
Yesterday's *Times* for sale.
The stationmaster in a green eyeshade
snoozing or dead.
Below the clock an American flag.
Twice a day empty trains
go by without stopping—
Eisenhower Eisenhower Eisenhower Eisenhower—
one-eyed trains twice a night—
FDR & FDR & FDR & FDR—
shuttle between
Albany Albany Albany Albany
Manhattan Manhattan Manhattan Manhattan

THE KNUTE ROCKNE STORY

Shouldn't the K be pronounced?
If not, his parents could have called him
Pnute, Gnute, Fnute, or Babbaganute.
His mother was toying with "Rock Knutne,"
but they decided on "Knute Rockne"
with a silent K.
If the Gipper's parents had done this
they could have named him the Kipper,
the Zipper, the Ripper, or the Dipper.
None of this happened
according to the movie.
I can never remember who the Gipper
was. Ronald Reagan? Iron Horseman?
I can barely remember Rock Knutne.
I loved football, and this is what it has done for me:
Thousands of letters lost in the mail,
our country's history an incomplete forward pass.

I WANTED TO BE A BALLERINA

No matter that I was a plump child, chickenbreasted,
with pigeon toes and goose flesh, it was the whirling
hippo in *Fantasia* that fired me for Terpsichore.
"But you're a boy," they said, "and have a swinish
case of psychosomatic gout to boot; give over
these hapless dreams." Friends, I speak to you tonight
as one who has conquered the quirks of circum-
stance and the incidents of birth. Laughter, pecker,
phlebitis of my left leg have been overcome by the
self-denial of toil; the thrifty sweat of industry has
manured my barren ground. Therefore I accept your
LL.D. with humility, but with pride. Thank you, Yale.
America, close your eyes and you will see me dancing.

MACHISMO

Apes, a bunch of them,
above them swinging
an old one
squeezing apeshots
at their heads
while each youngster
fights for fruit rinds,
looks upward respectfully,
snarls,
vomits and eats it,
scratches his neighbor's back,
or curiously inspects
his asshole.

Marilyn says
you can tell the junior faculty there,
Dan says
and the director of the corporation,
but I'm interested
in the solitary baboon in the corner,
who sits on his hands and waits,
growing stronger every day,
gazing vacantly
at the apes.

THE INHERITANCE

So, back to the lost paradise
after the neglect of fourteen years.
On the porch, at fourteen, I told my father
our condition resides within ourselves.
I had a red and white motorboat
to sail across the green-glazed patio
in autumn toward the wall of maples,
each golden on the edge of death.
Cousin Gunther sat on the patio
telling us secrets
and drinking
at noon; he knew the names of stars
and the proper name of toads,
and he is still alive somewhere,
a drunk repeating words to the green walls.
He was best at building giant snowmen
with basketball fists, and we
children, with round smoking mouths,
stood watching the old deciduous world,
in love with snowmen,
and never thought
that fourteen years away
we would still be standing,
arguing with prices in our mouths.
Little has changed
except for the dead.
The trees offer up their golden leaves
and a fat garden snake
squeezes into the dissolving wall.

AMONG HIS EFFECTS WE FOUND A PHOTOGRAPH

My mother is beautiful as a flapper.
She is so in love
that she has been gazing
secretly at my father
for forty years.
He's in uniform,
with puttees and swagger stick,
a tiny cork mustache
bobbing above a shoreline of teeth.
They are "poor but happy."
In his hand is a lost book
he had memorized,
with a thousand clear answers
to everything.

MY TEETH

The up-front ones are marvelous,
tiny dancers braving the wind,
shapely and disciplined.
But behind them, corruption,
molars who have lived riotously,
roots eaten by secret lusts
as their bodies disintegrate.
Even the bicuspids and incisors
are infected,
blood swollen
around stiff afflictions of plaque.

The stains of drugs and nicotine
have reached behind the skirts of the dancers
and it is only a matter of time
before the curtain comes down for good
and the closed mouth
fosters a strange revolution,
the muffled tongue rising
like a brutalized peasantry
to taste its own power
at last.

MY PENIS

Ordinarily I call it "my cock" but
often there is a strange formality about it,
this rocket with wattles.
"Penis" and "Vagina," a dignified couple
immobile on a Grecian urn
or at times engaged in elegant ballet and
desiring frequent medical checkups.
"Cock" and "Twat," two funloving kids
traveling from Pittsburgh to Tangiers
with a hundred bucks in their pockets,
laughing at Baptists but loving God.

Alone, it's
crazy and laughable, like the man
who stands up at every Quaker meeting,
testifying to his version of the Truth—
a drag to others but a private solace,
refusing to sit down when others whisper
"shush," "shame," "time and place for everything"—
a dotty old turkey continually rising in wonder,
even on lonely winter evenings refusing
not to point to the stars.

THE GIFT

One day
as I was lying on the lawn
dreaming of the Beautiful
and my wife was justifiably bitching out the window
at my shiftlessness and
the baby was screaming
because I wouldn't let him
eat my cigarettes,
a tiger cat leapt over the fence,
smiled at my wife,
let the baby pull his tail,
hummed like a furry dynamo
as I stroked him.

My wife took the car to get him some food,
my son began to sing his wordless song,
and I wrote a poem in the sand.

Now god give every man who's hopeless
a beautiful wife,
an infant son who sings
and the gift of a sweet-faced cat.

HOW TO GET HERE

The sun rises above the Expressway East;
follow that until noon.
At the fork in the road by the overturned semi,
go left, north by northwest.
A young woman with a lantern
will be seen walking along Route 156.
Follow her past a barn
with a broken reaper.
At a springhouse, go right
as the moon rises and past
an abandoned mineshaft.
Where the arrow for Old Route 210
points left, go straight up the hill
past the man with the shotgun
obliterating roadsigns.
At the top of the hill
there is an abandoned schoolhouse.
Inside is an elderly man in the dark
cataloguing antiques.
Be sure to approach him with a gift.
He has never met us but knows
we are here.

FACTS ABOUT DEATH

Richard Farina dove off a bridge at night in Ithaca
and six years later broke his neck by driving his
bike into a tree in California.

When my father died I remembered that one day in
a Chinese restaurant above the Ridgewood Theater
he sneezed chow mein.

I have been crying for six years about Farina.

I am about to buy a schoolhouse built in 1879. On
the foundation is scratched "DK." Bob Step, who will
sell it for $600, went to school there. Now he can't
get into it because of the bees.

I don't believe anything that Farina said. The Cuban
story, the peyote milkshake from the dark man. I think
Kristin was either the daughter of the Swedish am-
bassador or the girl from Alexandria with the mole
on her upper lip.

When he saw asparagus growing he said, "They look
like green pricks coming out of the earth." Farina
said, "The dead are trying to tell us something."

Outside the schoolhouse the pokeweed is growing.
In the fall their berries are dark as drops of old blood.
Poisonous. The old plant contains phytolaccin, caus-
ing paralysis, but also long used as a medicinal herb.

When they arise in the spring they look and taste like
asparagus.

The Elizabethans ripened apricots in dung and be-
lieved asparagus was an aphrodisiac, undoubtedly
because of the phallic suggestions.

The night Farina returned I got to make it with the girl
from Alexandria but, being drunk, couldn't get one
up. "Poor thing, poor thing, it's all right, I under-
stand," yawning.

My grandmother said, "You have to understand your
father." I've given it all up. When my mother found
him on the lawn he was serious as always. Cause of
death: digging weeds.

When I die I would like to be in that schoolhouse
among the poke plants, children and friends around
me, bees overhead, everybody laughing. I would like
to read them this and go underground laughing.

MIRACLE MILE

TOWARD THE SPLENDID CITY

> All paths lead to the same goal:
> to convey to others what we are.
> —*Neruda*

This is why in the wormpaths
of my solitary life
I want to grow cabbages,
with my thumb brush away
the tiny weeds, amaranth and purslane.

Do this early in the morning
before the birds are weary
or the sun bakes clay.
I remember how my grandmother
gave gifts of tomatoes and cucumbers,
picked the vegetables as the sun rose
and left them by doors
of silent houses.

If I could cultivate and water
the hearts of my children
I would do it,
my daughter strong and delicate
as fennel,
my son tough and moody as onions
upright in their solitude.

But there one works by indirection
in the strong heat of afternoons.
One hints and jokes,
loves by discussing the magnitude of suns
with a drink in one's hand,
or thudding softballs through the heavy air.

And in Pittsburgh,
where the blood of lost workers
haunts the soil beneath the pavement,
one afternoon I found beneath my office door
an anonymous note: "I love you."

Because we live this way I dream
of a whole people walking together
through their fields,
the work in common,
bodies touching,
eyes clear.

This is where one's fingers speak.
In the long rest after labor
a voice works through the fall streets
to meet its lover
beneath the white ring of ice.

FOR MY DAUGHTER

This is the summer storm,
soft rain and the dark,
the long lightning you murmur against
sleeping on the porch.
I carry you away from it,
sleeping, to your room.

And these are the steps of forgetfulness,
of leaving pain:
may honesty, the plain monkey
with a lost eye, never leave you;
may you have lovers numerous
as cardinals in the hemlock.
May they return forever.
May you hate fashion,
have the beauty of the potter's hands,
work in communities of friends.
And Whitman carried from the wreck
of my childhood:
"stand up for the poor
and the weak and the crazy."

These are the steps to the room
where parents are forgotten.
Because we die
I think of the story of the grass
that has lived forever
waving swords that can be cut
but come back and advance.

Because like any child
you sleep in the shell of your future
I stand with fists clenched, as rain
carries the sounds of your breathing away.

MIRACLE MILE

—for Gerald Stern

Why weep?
I am going to drive past Elby's Big Boy
and back, I am going to park beneath
the statue of Big Boy with his checkered pants
and his greasy cowlick like Reagan's,
I am going to admire his rosy cheeks
rounded as buttocks, and walk in to order
the minced veal parmesan. I am going to eat
garlic bread until the rich oil
runs down my jowls
and wipe my hands on dozens of paper napkins
insubstantial as dreams. I am going to think *Cafe Brulot*
as I drink a Coke and tip ten percent.
I am going to drive
past Cappelman's Discount Clothes
whistling Vivaldi and honk at the girls.
I am going to circle Our Lady of Perpetual Misery
lit by floodlights, and the crowd queuing up
at the Red Lobster to gobble Surf 'N' Turf
and drive past what may be a mugger humble
as Uriah Heep leaning against a Honda
in the outer dark of the parking lot at Sears.
I am going to walk into the Monroeville Mall
where George Romero shot *Night of the Living Dead*
and admire the heavy ironware in Horne's,
the electric woks and the microwaves,
the Dazey food strippers, the juice extractors
with automatic pulp ejectors,
the Wear-Ever popcorn poppers,
toaster ovens without end

and the kids walking the Walkman
around the Mall in a *paseo*
and shoplifting small goods—
a bra transparent as our prayers—
or palming packs of rubbers with the couple
on the package silhouetted by the evening sun.
I am going to admire the toucan in the Mall's aviary,
his beak the shape of a giant Brazil nut,
and be fitted for Harris tweed
at Hughes & Hatcher, where the cretinous salesmen
bob and slaver over my big roll of bills.
I'm going to chuckle at the basset hound
smoking a pipe in the Hush Puppies display—
she looks like a friend—and I am going to buy
chocolate pretzels at the Bavarian Haus.
I am going to drive past the Sheraton
more beautiful than any building in Japan.
I am going to follow the rumble and stink
of the garbage trucks into the dawn
and think of Camus, how he said he knew
with a certainty that our work is nothing
but the long journey to recover
through the detours of art
the two or three simple
great images which first
gained access to our hearts.

MONROEVILLE, PA

One day a kid yelled
"Hey Asshole!"
and everybody on the street
turned around

RETIRED MINERS

in Dr. Capelletti's office,
crippled and wheezing:

"if any guy   tells you
he got rich   through hard work
ask him   whose?"

ED SHRECKONGOST

The two of us roof my house,
canvas aprons weighted down
with tinned nails as we walk inchwise
on our knees across the grit of shingles.
Deciduous mountains, old men
sleeping, lie down all the way to Saltsburg,
here & there the unhealed scars of stripmines.
He keeps a pint in his pocket with the nails,
and late morning we sit astraddle
the ridge pole and pass whiskey back & forth:
"trouble with me is I ain't got an education
but I like my time free too—
you ain't work much, but you get by.
Same's me. 'Cept I'm what you call dog-poor,
got eighteen last count, costs more to feed
than kids. Some's belly always needs filled but—
She-it! last time the tax assessor come
ask me what I'm doin now, told'm
'Verne,
I'm a coonhunter,
presently
unemployed,'"
and laughs so hard his hammer
slips from his knee, slides the slant roof
and arcs out gracefully through air.

LEECHBURG, PA

One could almost be happy here.
The corner drugstore, Steinberg's,
like the fifties in Brooklyn
with a window full of surgical
appliances and pantyhose,
and in front on Friday night
a group of hoods
talking about getting laid maybe
but obviously not doing it,
their big dumb dicks
wrapped away like tubular chimes
on the symphony off-night,
like exclamation points
looking for something to happen
on Friday night, at Steinberg's
in Leechburg, Pennsylvania.

THE END OF THE ICE AGE

1

Because we smile so much
rice vanishes
from the wooden bowl of a child.

Because we smile so much
our heroes are guttering candles
fixed behind the sockets
of skulls.

It is because we smile so much
their wives wear leather coats
cut from our backs, sewn with waxed thread
thick enough to seal lips.

2

Alone, I hear myself say
"it is the end of the ice age."
The plants in their clay pots
tremble and nod, the wandering Jew
with its purple veins, the translucent impatiens,
the cut-tooth philodendron that whispers
as it's watered.

Upstairs, like a cloud defined
by its own gentleness, my wife sleeps;
from their distant dreams the children
occasionally cry out.

3

I remember faces I have never seen
across our loneliness. It is like a sudden tongue
of fire in dry wilderness bracken.
We feel it sometimes in the dreams of crowds
when music speaks through and for us.

Sometimes in the process of this night
we meet the obscure dead without speaking,
the hanged miner,
the old woman terrified in her room.
I think of a sodden mattress at the dump,
an ash tree bursting through it.
We have no single lives,
we are grass, trees,
hidden roots intertwined
mile upon mile.

BERTOLT BRECHT: ON THE INFANTICIDE, MARIE FARRAR

1

Marie Farrar. Birthdate: April.
No birthmarks, rickets, orphan, underage,
no known previous offenses. Claims
she murdered a baby thus:
she says that in her second month
she went to a woman in a basement apartment,
tried to abort by taking two douches.
Claims they were painful, but didn't work.

But you, I beg you, don't be angry at her.
Each creature needs the help of every other.

2

Nevertheless, she says, she paid what she owed,
and later laced her corset very tight,
also drank kerosene mixed with pepper
though her stomach couldn't hold on to that.
Her belly, visibly swollen, hurt her a lot
and cruelly when she washed the dishes.
At that time, she says, she was still growing.
She prayed to the Virgin Mary, hoped against all hope.

And you, I beg you, don't be angry at her.
Each creature needs the help of every other.

3

But her prayers apparently had no effect.
It was a lot to ask. When she grew bigger
she felt dizzy at morning mass. And she often sweated
from fear, frequently at the altar.
But she kept her condition secret
until the time actually arrived.

Who would believe that someone so plain,
so clumsy, fell victim to temptation.

And you, I beg you, don't be angry at her.
Each creature needs the help of every other.

4

On that day, she says, early in the morning
while washing stairs she felt as if nails
were clawing in her belly. She gets the shivers.
Yet she's able to keep the pain secret.
The whole day hanging out wash
she racks her brains, and then it hits her:
she's about to give birth, and right away
her heart is heavy. But she goes to bed quite late.

But you, I beg you, don't be angry at her.
Each creature needs the help of every other.

5

They woke her up again when she lay in bed:
Snow had fallen and she had to sweep it
till eleven. It was a long day.
But at night she could give birth in peace.
And later she bore, so she says, a son.
The son was a lot like other sons.
She was not a lot like other mothers,
though I have no cause to mock her.

And you, I beg you, don't be angry at her.
Each creature needs the help of every other.

6

I'll continue telling
what happened with that son
(she wanted, she says, to conceal nothing)
so that you can see what I am and what you are.
She says she was only in bed a short time
when strong pains struck her, and the only thing
she could think of—not knowing what would happen—
was to force herself not to scream.

And you, I beg you, don't be angry at her.
Each creature needs the help of every other.

7

Then with her last bit of strength, so she says,
since her room had grown ice-cold
she dragged herself to the servants' privy and there—
she doesn't know when exactly—gave birth
quietly. Maybe toward morning. She says
she was now confused, and so numb from cold
because snow could get into the room
that she could hardly hold the baby.

And you, I beg you, don't be angry at her.
Each creature needs the help of every other.

8

Between her room and the privy—before that,
she says, nothing happened—the baby began to cry
and that drove her crazy, she says,
and she hit it blindly with both fists and
couldn't stop until it was still, she says.

And then she took the dead thing up with her
to bed for the rest of the night
and in the morning hid it in the washhouse.

But you, I beg you, don't be angry at her.
Each creature needs the help of every other.

9
Marie Farrar. Birthdate: April.
Died in the penitentiary at Meissen,
unmarried mother, condemned, showing
the weakness of all creatures—
You who give birth in nice clean sheets,
you who call your impregnated bellies "blessed":
don't damn people lost and powerless;
if their sins were great, great also were their sorrows.

So, I beg you, don't be angry at her.
Each creature needs the help of every other.

THIS POEM IS FOR MARGARET

who picks apples
who climbs the long ladders
toward handfuls of fruit
who nests apples in canvas
rapidly without bruising them.
This poem is for Margaret
who comes from Minnesota
who says "the hardest work I ever done,"
who at the end of the day is perfumed with apples,
Black Gilliflower, Macoun, Winesap,
who disappears north with the harvest.

That is the direction of sorrow
and her laughter
slow and deliberate
as farm children.
Margaret, this poem is for going north
and for all those traveling
and for your eyes liquid
with the hard, red fruit.

KILLING RABBITS

Bend the neck back quickly
until it snaps,
cut off the head
close behind the skull.
Hang the carcass by a rear foot to bleed.
Skinning's easy: cut off the three loose feet
and tail with pruning shears, slit the fur
along the rear legs to the root of the tail
and pull off the pelt like a glove.
Cut through the skin of the belly,
the guts spill out of their little tub.
(I knew a man could clean a rabbit
by snapping the slit carcass like a whip.)

This is ugly. You wouldn't do it,
though you like to eat meat,
fat gravy made with the blood of steers,
sausages stuffed with the brains of pigs.

You were always delicate,
averting your eyes in Florida
as your Buick purred by the migrants,
ten people in a tin-roof hut.
You were happy, years ago, when you got
to the bridge without crossing Harlem.
Even the steelworkers flowing like a dark river
oppress you; you ride past J & L
forcing your hands
to leave the windows open.
In the supermarket you shrink
from bloodwater in the plastic trays,
though your appetite is healthy.
In the silence of your well-policed rooms
your capped teeth flash and tear flesh.

110 YEAR OLD HOUSE

Betsy, if erasers could sing
they'd sound like your finches,

the only birds I've seen that seem
to like being caged, in their little pagoda

croaking like miniature geese
to the Jackson Browne that Ned's taping

for his report on stripmines
and to the sound of the grackles

that live in the attic.
To them, everything's music.

And to me, snoozing with my flu,
watching the machines crawl the stripmine

in back of the Schmeltzers';
I'm so lazy today even the muffled thump

of the miners' dynamite
and the rattling of the loose window make sense

and you most of all, yelling in the kitchen
"my finches, I must say hello to my finches"

and running up the stairs
with your 11 year old feet

so hard that the whole old house trembles
and then the slam of your door

and a chorus of finch honks which, as you say,
is just their way of saying hello

to you, to us, to our cages.

"ARVIDA KLINGENSMITH WOULD LIKE TO INVITE YOU TO CHURCH"

Rural Methodist, 83 members, 12 children,
4 young adults. Sermon this Sunday on the text:
"the greatest unexplored space
is the one beneath your hat."
Rat discovered in the combination
bathroom/vestry last week after
the head of the Shelocta Beekeepers
testified on "Thrift."

Every Sunday in nice weather, from the porch
Ed Shreckongost lifts his beercan
in salute as his wife the organist
backs out the old Blazer and growls off
beneath a halo of smoke,
and the oldest parishioner, 103,
is carried in dozing by his great-grandsons,
and every Sunday the wealthy chiropractor/
stripmine operator stands witness
to the Truth, as when he announced
that celebrating Halloween was pagan

so that last year 12 kids,
unmasked, disrobed and grumbling,
were herded to an "All Saints party"
in the basement
(no pumpkins, no apple bobbing,
no screwing around)
but afterward, goofy with laughter,
hurled themselves out among
the ancient stones, the rows
of ancestral Klingensmiths and Shreckongosts
and Schmeltzers leaning against the wind
as the thin finger of the clapboard steeple
stood firm against the moon.

AFTER THE SUMMER PARTY

How silvery the peach tree is
out the bathroom window at 7 am
a copy of O'Hara's *Selected Poems*
on the floor near the toilet
and Britt gives me a cup of coffee
this is the life I'm tired
of thinking about whether I'm any good
or not or what happened to the Pirates this year
I like those peach trees
even if they haven't yielded fruit yet
God, I can see my father disapproving
as I clean up the bottles and the ashes
like dandruff all over the table
his big nose pinched white
so what? did he ever make $400 an hour?
"the lights just went out!" yells Britt
"so what?" I say "they just went back on"
who needs light at 7 am?
I remember seeing his play
The General Returns from One Place to Another
at the Writers Stage with Britt and Levine
and that was a warm day too
though it was night
what's for breakfast?
fresh raspberries and yogurt
there's a fly trapped at the screen
why not help it escape?
I'm going to sit here all day
like the chameleon we had in Florida
slowly turning gold on the fence
feeding on air
lapping dew

COOKING

Peel the shrimp, cut the pak choi
on the bias, shred the peppers.
If you wipe the mushrooms
I'll slice them with the chef's knife,
cut the pale breast of chicken into matchsticks,
the mild onion into rings,
start the oil smoking in the pan;
sesame oil is better,
but you can use safflower.

I love you & I'm gabbling & cutting
because I think you're happy too.
Give me a plate. I'll pour wine,
the hell with the thin glasses,
a cup will do.

When I was young I was tongue-tied
and I can't remember when the men
  in my family
didn't sit, stare at their plates
and shovel, silent as though they'd learned
they'd just contracted syphilis.
And the women, who cooked for love,
beamed.

I think that's why I learned to cook,
so my hands would have something to do.
It's not that they didn't have words,
it's that they didn't trust them.
I mean my hands, and my father and uncles.
They never read *Gatsby*, but they believed in him.
They wanted to make money, to take their rich shirts

out of the drawer and spill them across the bed
so someone would say, "what beautiful,
what beautiful shirts." It was cleaner
than talking, or cooking, if you could never
say anything gracefully.

So I learned to love steamy windows, and
I can cook better than my mother.
I can talk better than my father.
And I've always loved pouring wine,
twist it off neatly, or if there's nothing better
put a big jug of Gallo on my shoulder
and without spilling a drop
glug out shots in a cup.
I like my voice and hands.
Over dinner, they meet your hands.

THE GOOD-BYE, FAREWELL, AUF WIEDERSEHEN POEM

—for Gar

We are all driving to the house of god
in the dark. Yes, and the long lashes
of my windshield wipers brush the tears
from the curved glass: hush, hush,
deep into this night, and wonderful:
the prudent asleep in their tiny houses,
the sorrow of paperwork limp on their desks
and wonderful the hum and plash of the rubber
on the wet roads and the distance
from the sleeping ego, that grackle
with its *I, I, I, I.*
Not the distance from, but the traveling to
effortless as the car's glide
down the S-curve outside Apollo
over the rumbly steel waffle of the Kiski Bridge
to the small lights of the empty town,
a single figure leaning on a column
at the one hotel. And the rain.

May we only ever be lonely
by choice, driving to a bubble of light
and to sleep, and in the morning
the strong rinsed sun on the floor,
on the table the dark iris
in the consolation of its old vase.

CHANGING THE NAME TO OCHESTER

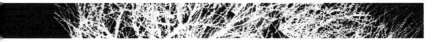

PACKING LUNCH

Of course I'd rather have Crab Louis
or *Moules à la Provençale* or Shrimp Mornay,
or Flavio's fettucini carbonara—
though what with the fresh cream and
home-cured bacon I'd be digging
my own grave with my teeth—or even
skirt steak, which Bob Watt called
a little sexy for Milwaukee, but all that
would be violating what Thoreau said
about being rich in inverse proportion
to one's needs; and besides, if I hadn't
bagged my lunch I wouldn't have gone
to Roy Rogers to buy a Diet Coke and
slip a few free tomato slices
into a napkin and heard two grad students
arguing, one saying "I'm perfectly willing
to discuss laissez-faire capitalism
in a rational way if you'd *please*
stop impugning my mother," and maybe
I wouldn't have felt free to call London
($1.76 a minute, direct dial) to say hello,
me not too far from where
Braddock in His Majesty's Service
got wiped in the French and Indian Wars
and twenty miles from where Colonel Armstrong,
"the hero of Kittanning," returned the favor
by slaughtering Delawares on Blanket Hill
which is now an abandoned speedway
covered by weeds, and if I didn't have the time—
which is everything—I couldn't reread Proust,
as Reynolds Price says he's doing this summer,
because he's willing to make "the all-but-endless
concessions of time, attention, and boredom"
Proust demands, though maybe I don't want

to reread Proust, maybe I just want to dream
today about Coney Island when I was a kid,
and Steeplechase hadn't been torn down and
how you entered it through a huge rolling barrel
where almost nobody could stand up and
as the bodies slid around and on top
of one another enormous mechanical laughter and
static crackled from the loudspeakers, but it was ok,
you crawled out and stood up again and smiled,
but the only thing left of Steeplechase
is the giant Parachute Ride, dead for years
and looking like the Eiffel Tower in the midst
of Paris bombed though I remember riding
The Cyclone for the fourth time in a night
with my father who was turning green but
who told my mother "I can't let the boy
ride something as dangerous as this by himself"
so that while we rode she stood anxious, peering
up at the roller coaster cars clattering
on the rickety track all around her,
as outside the vendors sold boiled corn from
sidewalk vats, and the goony sailors alive
home from Korea walked their girls up and down
the boardwalk, singing and talking dirty and
the smells of unhealthy food everywhere—
frozen chocolate bananas, and rainbow
cotton candy and hot Italian sausage
blanketed in cheese on a bun—and later,
snacking at Nathan's Famous, the ambulances whining
past on Coney Island Avenue and the Famous
Irish Tenor singing in the bar next door,
my father told me how Luna Park had burned down
when he was a kid, and how Luna Park

(I thought: "luna moths") made Steeplechase
look like nothing;

o love, I'm going on
because first images are clearer,
or maybe it's that in early memories
everyone is still alive, and maybe
that's what Freud misunderstood in his strictures
on "the oceanic feeling" and maybe that's why
I've already spent time today talking to Ted Weesner
who's going to that writers' conference in Maine
and is smiling about it, though they have him listed
as a poet rather than a fiction writer
which is ok, he probably should be a poet
though his movie options would be a lot less,
and why I told him how I used to spend time on the Cape
when I was 20, gathering mussels from the rocks
in the tide pools to steam with a little
white wine and parsley and basil for my friends
some of whom are gone, and afterwards
smoke cigars and watch the breakers rolling—
"why don't you count the sand?" my mother
said once at the beach when I was six or seven—
and to tell the truth, I'm thinking *time*
a lot lately, and about what's necessary,
and even more since this morning when Dave
agreed with me about a mutual friend,
that there's no use talking about it
or devising strategies or travelling to China,
if you want to write you just sit your ass
down in a chair and begin to type, though
of course it's more than just that, it's
studying as I did last night a silver siliqua

of the Emperor Gratian, that unlucky, dead
handsome man, gone nearly 1700 years, who
was too busy and too miserable to love,
though I'm not sure what "love" means
if it doesn't have the luxury of a life's
memory, which of course is too dangerous
for any of us to ride by ourselves; and
I guess it's what I'm thinking just now,
how Hugo told me a year before he went back
on the sauce, that "it's amazing how much work
you get done when you stop drinking," and
I guess it's because he drank a bit
that I'm thinking too about Doctor Breslau,
that good man, our dentist, who ministered
to the poor and got mugged for it, and who
lent me once when I was very young
three books by Shaw—and of course because
irony is very cheap and omnipresent
Heartbreak House was one of them—
and had a collection of skulls
from digs in Mexico in his waiting room
and would happily discuss the various kinds
of dental caries manifest in each, and how
at my birth he gave my parents
a ten dollar gold piece for me,
which I sold when I was in high school
to get money for a date, so that
I have nothing left from him and
I am beginning to weep and
I am writing the first draft of this
as much as I can
on a plain brown paper bag.

WEEHAWKEN FERRY

The bulletnosed cars lined up behind
the bluntnosed cars; the men who
cast the hawsers off were redfaced
in the cold and spat and spat. Goodbye
New York. Everybody wore fedoras or
little pillboxes with feathers. Hello
Jersey. Always in the river clots
of brown foam, orange peels, rotted wood
chipped from the spongy piers. Green
paint chipping off rails, over there
the green woman with the torch. Huge
sexual trembling of the screws positioning
the hulk in its slip. Motors coughing on,
and the slow crawl past bills: Ray
Bolger, *Charlie's Aunt*, *Oklahoma*, Ike,
Ike, Ike, Ike, Ike, and the old car
climbed the switchback carved
into the lordly Hudson's Palisades,
slipping on the cobbles and the brown ice.
At the crest the Sunday stillness of
gray frames, Ike, Ike, here and there
a new pair of shoes with leather soles
and heels walked slowly the iced sidewalks.

THE CANARIES IN UNCLE ARTHUR'S BASEMENT

In the white house in Rutherford
the ancient upright piano never worked
and the icy kitchen smelled of Spic and Span.
Aunt Lizzie's pumpkin pie turned out green
and no one ate it but me and I did
because it was the green of the back porch.
That was the Thanksgiving it rained and I first thought
of rain as tears, because Aunt Lizzie was in tears
because Arthur came home from the soccer game drunk
and because he missed dinner brought a potted plant
for each female relative, and walked around the table
kissing each one as Lizzie said "Arthur, you
fool, you fool," the tears running down her cheek as
Arthur's knobby knees wobbled in his referee's
shorts, and his black-striped filthy shirt wet from the rain
looked like a convict's. What did I know?
I thought it meant something. I thought
no one would ever be happy again. I thought
if I were Uncle Arthur I'd never again
come out from the dark basement where he raised canaries,
the cages wrapped in covers Aunt Lizzie sewed,
and where, once, when I was very small and because Uncle Arthur
loved me or loved his skill or both he slowly removed the cover
from a cage and a brilliant gold bird burst into song.

THREE WHITE KIDS SINGING DOO-WOP

What did I ever need besides
my blue modified pegged pants
with the white saddle stitches and
a skinny black belt, and Bobby Tarantino,
the drummer, with his black boots with the real
sharp spic heels, and George Cava in pants
so tight he needed "a shoehorn to get into them,"
waiting in the sunlight in spring
in front of the Bohack store
on Myrtle Avenue for the bus
to take us to school, while we do little shuffle
steps and dips and sing in the strong sun?
What does anybody really need?

Doo-wop a bam sham boom sha bam.

WORKING AT THE WHOLESALE CURTAIN SHOWROOM

"Can you type?" Jake said.
"Maybe ten words a minute."
"That's ok," Jake said, "we just get
a couple letters now and then,
what we need is a smart kid to be nice
to customers, you don't have to know nothin
about curtains, just be nice when people
come through the door, talk nice to the buyers
you don't have to know nothin about curtains
just show them the way to the samples,
we got all the stuff, the styles, the prices,
printed on the cards. What we need is a nice
educated kid, like you, you'll do fine."

And I did, and this is in praise of Jake,
may he have prospered, who paid me for nothing,
and who knew the great secret of living:
"be nice," and who once sent me with roses
to the apartment of a female buyer
with the warning: "this is a fine lady,
look around and tell me what the place
looks like, you can tell a lot about people
from the look of their place," and I came back
and said "she's got a nice place, and she's really
pretty, and she's got a full set of the Yale Shakespeare
books in her living room," and Jake said "oh shit,
I'll never get anywhere with her
if she's an intellectual."

HARVEY'S ASS

What he liked about the Stones' "Sweet Virginia"
was "got to scrape the shit right off your shoes"
and he'd wiggle his ass like Jagger which was
unfortunate since though Jagger's ass has been
called in print "two collar buttons" and
"a knife-edged ass" when I heard
Harvey mumble "right offf yr
shoes" I'd see his rear
swing like a monstrous
clapper without a bell,
like two pillows in pants,
like a pair of fleshy
wrecking balls in
dissynchronous dance but
that was a long time ago and he might
be dead by now, or a Libertarian, or addicted
to the Southampton Diet, and hey at least
he heard some music
and he moved.

DUKE

It took him years to get out of the mailroom
at Whitehead Metals but he did it,
made 70 bucks a week in posting,
and though he finally got his figures neat
he always had trouble remembering which was sheet and
which was slab, and confused the ID's of pipe with OD's,
and sometimes stared at the numbers on the PO's
in his ham fists for minutes before
he subtracted the poundage from the cards.

One day when the boss was out Jackie Olson yelled
"Hey—Duke took the Mrs. to a movie last night,
The Ten Commandments. How'd you like it Duke?
D'ja understand what it was about?"
And we waited while Duke turned his huge head
like a buffalo with its horns down and said
"yeah, I liked it, it was about
da beginning a da Catlic religion.
Up yours."

THE BOSS

was a swivelchair of flab slowly sucking
smoke from a corncob who wanted respect,
who wanted to be called "Mr. Ciccatano"
or "Boss," which he probably would have been
if his long protruding lips hadn't resembled
Dopey's in *Snow White*, and when the older guys
called him "Sam" he pretended not to hear,
though it wasn't just his looks but that
when Mr. Grover, the Big Boss, staggered
back from lunch at 2:00 the Boss stood
to attention as though the flag,
drenched in martinis, was going by
and the anthem in the background
was muffled giggles and some sucking noises
which he pretended not to hear but
sat down to stare into space and dream,
his pipe sending up periodic smoke clouds
as monuments to ambition, and
every afternoon he straightened
his tie in the john, put on
his sharkskin jacket and
walked out alone.
Duke swore the Boss
went once a week to the hookers on Bleecker,
and that must have cost him too, forced
to hock whatever dignity he had left
in the tiny pawnshop of the groin.

THE WHITEHEAD METALS STICKBALL TEAM
AT LUNCH HOUR ON W. 10th ST.

Duke, like a gorilla
with a stripped branch in his hand,
tongue stretching in concentration to his nose,
could hit the Spauldeen pinkball into the Hudson.
Harry the Head, the nervous macrocephalic
who was your friend forever if
you bought him a shot of Cutty Sark,
was a scooter but had lousy hands.
And Jackie Olson the Ivy Leaguer
who took one course a term at night
at Columbia, played wearing one
of his three or four ties from Chipp's,
and Ronald from the warehouse
led the cheers—"le's see you fuckers
hit the ball for once"—and Tony Sciotto
who had five kids and $70 a week laughed,
always, when he ran the bases.

Thomas said "it all happens
in a flash of light," that's right
and whenever I remember those words
I think of a baseball field in August, a few gulls
floating over the bright green
as Parker hits a grand slam against LA,
or that poor street where nothing ever happened
except trucks hauling sheet and slab and
at lunch that motion and yelling,
everyone in a momentary pure relation
with everybody else, and the filthy river's
gulls floating over, the joy of movement
as the sun looks down on the poor and the great

as it did on the soldiers crawling up the beach at Anzio
or on the Enola Gay in the serene
dozing its way to Hiroshima
or on the great Emperor Maximin, killed
in his tent by his troops, in June.

We're godlike in our capacity to forget.
Hey listen, once it happens, it's gone.
And don't kid yourself, when you're happy you're happy.
Don't kid yourself, when you're dead you're dead.

I don't know what happened to any of them.
I remember Jackie Olson, the smart one, was promoted
to salesman, and I remember him rigid with happiness,
bouncing up and down in his swivel chair.
The night before Harry the Head joined the army
I bought him a Scotch at the White Horse;
he got in just in time for Vietnam.

There's so much pain you're a fool
for talking about it. But what's amazing
is how those in pain think it's normal.
What's wonderful is that it never changes:
how the damned laugh and sing when they can,
how the years change everything to gold.

THE RELATIVES

Holidays, I'd look out the window for them
gathering like a flock of black-coated birds:
at Christmas, Fat Charlie, all red-faced and boozy,
who always told jokes about outhouses and
parted his sparse hair down the middle;
crippled Marie, who didn't want to be a bother,
and Uncle George, the fierce fire chief and
Evelyn Number One with her warbling voice;
Lotte of the high Hungarian cheekbones,
who was beautiful and pious, and Uncle Arthur
who did not always know where he was but is
the only one left of the old ones, 94 this week.

I want to name them all before they go utterly,
young women with gold at their breasts,
the men in their pride and small schemings,
songs after drink and the gossip,
old stories late into the night
as they praised their dead
as best they could, absolving
themselves with their repetitions
for never having had adequate words,
becoming thus, though clumsy,
like the *scop* in the meadhall,
like Nestor in the Pylian camp,
rescuing something from death, for the young,
for me eating cakes with ginger ale,
listening, and it was all new:
the immigrants sailing in steerage to the New World—
"the ocean is big" my grandmother said,
who spent her whole life washing clothes—
the German builder of the bakery in Kingston,

the Wife Who Died From Grief When Her Husband Died,
the Son Who Supported His Mother and Three Brothers.

I never understood their sadness, I felt
a generation too late, at the edge of the world,
and when they left and walked out into the black
and under the street lamps on Woodhaven Blvd.
it was as though they were walking through spotlights
the way Jimmy Durante did on television
at the end of the program slowly walking,

his back bent, from spotlight to spotlight
stopping at each to turn and wave and
walk again into an infinite regression
of lights, turning and waving,
kissing goodbye.

All I have left are a few stories
and an image of a long parade,
George and Sybil, Charles, Ernest
who always smelled of kerosene,
little people joining the famous
in shrinking as they go backward
through the abyss with the others,
older, all traveling: Ruprecht,
Harthacnut, Wang-Wei, and before them,
Arzes, Sextus Marcius, waving and bowing,
Praxithea, Agathocles, an immense crowd
kissing and walking away
until each is tiny as
one neuron
or gone.

CHANGING THE NAME TO OCHESTER

When other grandpas came to Ellis Island
the Immigration people asked "Name?"
and they said "Sergius Bronislaus Jygzywglywcz"
and the officer said "ok, from now on your name's
Sarge Jerko," and Sarge trundled off to the Lower East Side
with a lead cross and a sausage wrapped in a hair shirt
and shared a tiny ill-lit room with eight *Landleute*
and next to a pot of boiling diapers began to carve
yo-yos to peddle on the street and forty years later
was Sarge Jerko, Inc., the Yo-Yo King,
but my grandfather who was born in this country
(no one living knows anything about *his* parents)
and was an engineer for Con Edison
when he married the immigrant girl
Katherina Humrich who everybody said
was once very pretty but when I knew her
had a tight bun, thin German lips
and a nose which came to her chin;
her major pleasures were trips to Coney Island
with friends and frightening little children
by jumping out from behind curtains, after which
she cackled hilariously. This is all I know for certain
about my grandfather: 1) his name was Olshevski,
and he changed it shortly after his marriage,
when they were living in an Irish neighborhood,
2) while working at Con Ed he bought a yacht
my grandmother said, but my mother said "Mom,
it was just a boat," 3) he left Katherina
after the fourth son was born, and she lived
in a tiny apartment on Chauncy Street
which smelled, even when I was eight,
like boiled diapers, 4) he was reported

to be handsome and have "a roving eye,"
5) my father and his brothers
all of whom are dead now
refused to go to his funeral
and never spoke of him.

This is a poem about forgiving Grandpa
for my not knowing him. And father, if you're
reading over my shoulder, I don't forget how
you had three cents spending money a week
and gave two cents to the church, or how
Uncle George, the baby who was everybody's
darling, couldn't go to college because he had
to work to support the family like everybody else
and how he became a fire chief in the City of New York,
and how Uncle Will, before he died of cancer,
became an advisor to LaGuardia and made a bundle
by being appointed trustee of orphans' estates,
or how Uncle Frank, driving his battery truck
once was stopped by Will and LaGuardia in their big car
and they chatted, and Uncle Frank—my favorite uncle,
neither Olshevski nor Ochester—still talks
about how his partner Paddy kept saying
"Bejasus, it was the Mayor,"
or how because you had to support your brothers
you couldn't marry till 30
and were engaged for eight years to my mother
who to this day loves you because you did
what you had to do, and how you built your business
going door-to-door selling insurance on Chauncy Street
and Myrtle Avenue till late at night, arguing and collecting
quarters and dimes from people who lived in tiny apartments

smelling of boiled diapers.
Nearly twenty years since your death, father,
and long ago I've forgiven you, and I think
you did love me really, and who am I, who was born
as you said "with everything," to condemn
your bitterness toward your father who left you
as you said "with nothing"?

I don't believe in original sin.
I believe if we're strong enough and gather our powers
we could work it out: no petty human misery,
no windrows of the dead slaughtered
in suicide charges, no hearts shrunken
and blackened like meat spitted
and held too long to the fire.
But what everybody knows
is enough to make you laugh
and to break your heart.
Grandpa, forty years after your death,
by the power vested in me as the oldest
living Ochester in the direct line I hereby
forgive you. And though you died,
my mother says, penniless and alone
with no one to talk to
I hope that when you abandoned your family
you lived well. I hoped you sailed your 15-foot
yacht out into Long Island Sound
with a pretty woman on board and a bottle
of plum brandy. I hope that when the huge yacht
with "Jerko II" on the stern sailed by
you looked up and said "honey,
you'll be sailing one like that some day"

and that she giggled and said "yeah,
hon, gimme a kiss" and afterwards tilted
the bottle, and that the sun was shining
on the Sound, and that you enjoyed
the bitter smell of the brine and
the brilliance of the white scud and
that when you made love that night
it was good and lasted
a long, long time.

CONVERSATION WITH ARTUR SCHNABEL

John Cage sucks
though we mustn't say so.
When I first heard "prepared piano"
I thought of deveined liver—
little slices squeezed into the strings—
or prepared mustard, little red flags
of French's waving us on toward tiny thrills:
"Oh Edna, I think I'm going to throw up!"
At least Telemann and Neil Young aren't
entirely predictable. Ever since the war
Charles Ives makes me ill with his collages,
the little white towns in Vermont
with their orange autumn obbligatos,
the uniformed band blowing snatches
of military marches as above it all
my chopper leans over for the strafe run.
The found poem's a hundred years old
and tv quick-cuts better than Eliot.
The only thing I don't get tired of
is the heart, the way it moves
down the highway like a '47 Hudson,
that tank-like car, the tires massive
and the radio blaring, as it was years ago
when my parents drove into the great night
of upstate New York, my erection
in the back seat uncontrollable,
though I couldn't say so,
my lights flashing, all my flags flying
toward the wars.

Of course
we like "the great control"
of art because ordinarily we're hapless,
all our thrills to come,
like the redneck soldier stumbling
through Times Square, dressed to kill
with his Purple Heart on.

WALKING AROUND THE FARM

This is where I shot the rabbit
from the back porch
when we first moved in
but found it inedible,
covered with fleas. This
is where we made love
in the woods, surrounded by ferns,
our asses bitten by mosquitoes.
This is where our daughter, age 6,
was tossed like a tenpin
by a running bulldog.
This is the black walnut tree
beneath which we drank beer
the morning Nixon resigned.
This is where years ago
I grew reefer among the corn.
This is the gravestone
so weathered we can't read the name.
This is where Roger parked
his Volkswagen the night he came back
from Vietnam and we listened
to Van Morrison in the rain
all night delicately sipping Jim Beam.
This is where the crabapple tree fell
during the great wind of '79.
This is the mailbox
where the postman, Mr. John,
picks up his two dozen eggs a week.
This is where we picked the lambsquarters
that sustained us in our first year.
That's where I sit in good weather
when I'm thinking a poem.

That is the road that runs
into the black woods
where my daughter, age 12,
saw something running through the brush
that she said seemed almost human, but huge,
naked and terrified.

THE COIN DREAM

Betsy said "in my dream
there was a huge pool of water
in the backyard and I was diving
for coins, there were coins everywhere
and whenever I dove I found beautiful ones,
old Greek coins with swans and doves.
Ned found a coin that you said was rare
and priceless, but whenever I dove
I found coins you said were beautiful
and that you would always treasure.
That dream was so real I still know
where I found the most wonderful ones,
under the big maple root
near the clothesline. There was one
with a lady in a helmet
holding a spear and a shield
that looked like the moon. Tomorrow
I'm going out there to see if the dream
was telling me something."
And I said, "it was."

POEM FOR A NEW CAT

Watching her stand on the first
joints of her hind legs like a kangaroo
peering over the edge of the bathtub
at my privates floating like a fungoid lilypad,
or her bouncy joy in pouncing on a crumpled
Pall Mall pack, or the way she wobbles walking
the back of the couch, I think when
was it we grew tired of everything?
Imagine the cat jogging, terrified
that her ass might droop, or studying
the effective annual interest paid
by the First Variable Rate Fund, the cat
feeling obliged to read those poems that
concentrate the sweetness of life like prunes.
OK, that's ridiculous—though the cat
also kills for pleasure—but I find
myself in the middle of the way,
half the minutes of my sentient life
told out for greed and fear.
The cat's whiskers are covered with lint
from the back of the dryer.
                              Friend,
how it is with you I don't know
but I'm too old to die.

THE LATIN AMERICAN SOLIDARITY
COMMITTEE FUNDRAISING PICNIC

"What we'd like to do" he said
"is include some local poets
in the entertainment."
"Sure" I said.
It was at the Mellon Pavilion
in Frick Park and when I got there
they were running late. "Listen"
he said "I'm really sorry,
the poetry has to go later in the program
because we still haven't raffled off
the bottle of Cuban rum."
"Sure" I said.
After the Cuban rum there was an interlude
with mariachi music and solo guitar and
then a professor of sociology
gave a full account of his recent
trip to Cuba and how the Cuban people
despite having just broken the ubiquitous
chains of American economic imperialism
showed unfailing courtesy to visiting dignitaries
such as himself.
By this time it was almost dark.
"Jeez" he said "if we have the poetry now
we'll never get in any volleyball."
"That's ok" I said "I like volleyball."
So I played, and the other team was pretty good.
I got three balls spiked in my face.
After that I drank some beer and talked
with a pretty Mexican woman.
After the beer ran out I went home.

Under cover of darkness
the revolution was gathering steam.

POEM FOR BASHO

If I am timorous and
hesitant to intrude
on your privacy,

forgive me, for though
every poet in New York
has written a poem to you

it is different here
where one farm does not wish
to violate another

farm's solitude, but
if after 300 years you
were in this valley

perhaps you would write
about the mouse who
every night travels out

to eat at the dog's dish.
And I think you would like
the wind stunted spruce

and the way the drip, drip
of the sink gathers
the night around it.

Basho, here is my yellow glass.
I am alone, but happy because
I do not have to be alone.

You understand that, surely?
How one of the pleasures
of silence is finally

returning to your friends.
Even though, no doubt, they thought
you slightly peculiar.

What are the colors of flowers
at night? And Basho, will you
have another glass of rice wine

or whiskey? Basho, may
I show you a poem I've just written?
Basho, what are 300 years?

MARY MIHALIK

She'd tried to kill herself before.
Six kids, no money.

She was drunk
they said, doing 80, 90

on the slick blacktop
twisty and at dusk, and they

said there were no skidmarks
where she sailed under

the coal truck going slow
uphill out of the crossroad and

sheared the top of her Chevette
clean off and the rumor was

that when the cops came,
in the back seat they found her head.

People said all she needed
was a job, and I guess they're right.

And probably everyone thought
she needed love but everybody

says you've got to earn that,
though I think love's a gift,

the way money is for some, who
have a lot and never earned it.

I don't know. But a few nights later
when I walked past there, the insects

were at their cheerful static.
Aside from them the woods were silent.

And there were fireflies.

NEW DAY

Yes, the sun rises an angry red,
what the Romans called *oriens*,
what the religious associate with Christ,
and I walk out in my shorts, stretching
and puffing to train the scarlet runner beans
to their trellis; whatever god governs
beans has smiled, the vines grown
a foot overnight, and as I lace them
around the nervous network of twine
my son, who last night collapsed
in an anguish of stertorous breathing
comes down, stretches and yawns, pees.
Pots rattle in the kitchen,
grits and eggs,
and the rooster with a pneumonic lung
croaks—oohgggHHH—for the sun
but he hasn't died yet and
as I'm eating, the radio says
the President is lobbying
to subvert another small country
and I flip the dial and a preacher
who knows nothing says that except
for one thing there is nothing to know,
and when I walk out again
a hummingbird's in the salvia,
the sun's up, the dog on his chain
whines for breakfast, and the squash
are flourishing and when I stand near them
with my bright yellow shirt the cucumber beetles,
who love anything yellow, land on me and
are destroyed, sinners on the shirt
of a jealous god, and the sun's rising
to zenith, the chickens are scratching

around in their mud and if you
were very young you could say
this is heaven what with the dew
and the birds chirpy and all and yes
if you wait long enough
you will see the new moon
with the old moon in her arms.

POEM WRITTEN FOR THE FIFTH ANNIVERSARY
OF THE THREE RIVERS SHAKESPEARE FESTIVAL

The thing he knew most about us was that we dream
our lives, until pain or love awaken us, and so
in this theater we are most alive. Sometimes
when the play is over and I walk out onto Forbes,
back into the little O of our world,

I think of the great Elizabeth, of her young court
compact of music, dance and more lovers
than Belmont held, how finally the music fled and,
her heart failing, in late age she killed her last
lover, Essex; the lonely queen in an absurd red wig;

and I watch the lovers walking down Forbes at night
to their own unexpected destinies, and the solitary
figures rapidly going somewhere, and the lights of the city,
and I know that the certainties in our tentative hearts
are upheld by words alone, as for instance Portia, who

by her hard gaiety holds the whole rotten edifice
of Venice up. And after the play I want to talk to friends,
I want to be part again of the bright coming and going

in the dark, as Shakespeare was in his great city,
which is ours, with the same eternal gossip of the heart,
the same characters walking the long streets,

the same miracle of some humans dreaming
"not the smallest orb which thou behold'st
but in his motion like an angel sings."

BLIZZARD, DECEMBER 2

My son calls to say his plane arrived
safely in Chicago and he's in his overheated room

but on tv I see Green Bay playing in a blizzard
that's moving east, the first flakes perhaps

hissing in the Chicago River, swirling around
the Art Institute blacked out on a Sunday night,

then moving into Indiana, smothering the motel
in Valparaiso where a quarter century ago

I made love to a girl I hardly knew and later
we both cried in the bar at the thought of parting

because at that age one is the most romantic
or stupid, because one wants to be

and everything should last, including
the pretty illusions of permanence,

and now the snow is covering the great dead
U.S. Steel works at Gary and gathering itself

in fury to cover the tiny hills, small as
burial mounds, around Elkhart where last summer

I had dinner in a good place with fresh oysters
when I was dead tired and the waitress

asked if I knew how Captain Hook had died
— "crotch itch!" she said, roaring—and then the snow

with nothing to stop it whistles into Ohio
and the Turnpike shuts down except for the plows

with eerie lights flashing cruising the wastes
and Cleveland goes under and I hope Bob Wallace

is safe and warm and has plenty of brandy
for his Alexanders and the storm descends

on Akron where Elton is still a little melancholy
again for not getting the job back home in New Orleans

and then into the foothills of the Alleghenies
and in Pittsburgh the travellers coming in

from the airport will exit the tunnel above downtown
and see the first flakes settling and the beautiful lights

and say "shit" and prepare to slide down the terrible hills
as always and I hope all of my friends are home

looking out at the night as the huge flakes
descend, as they say on tv, "in earnest,"

and not out on the black streets with the cars
slipping sideways, and the snow moves east

and begins to coat our country roads and
the township's two-man road crew say

"damn" at midnight and get up and begin
to cruise the dirt roads with their twenty

year old plow, and kids have been staring at snow
against the barn lights and hoping no school for a week and

not thinking about all the natural associations
of snow with death and separation or how

in the morning the snow will be a foot deep
on the bales of hay covering the carrots

in the garden, the golden spikes shrinking
from the cold the way that the penises

even of football players do, and it is
the season of death, though if everyone you love

is ok and the smoke curls from the lost chimneys
of houses in the next valley you can bear it,

and tomorrow morning, the first day of deer season,
I will be out on the porch sniffing the air

and grumbling, and go inside where my books
are sleeping on their shelves, and my guns

are sleeping on their racks because I don't
hunt now, though outside men are rejoicing

because you can track a wounded deer
by its trail of blood in the snow, but

what I'm thinking about most is that my son
is walking around as they dig out in Chicago

and that everything is safe again in the deep earth
and that nothing in the system right now can hurt us.

FOR THE ZOROASTRIANS

"the religion was concerned...with protecting and
treating kindly domestic animals"
—*The New Columbia Encyclopedia*

Nietzsche, who knew a thing or two,
preferred *Zarathustra*, as closer to the Persian,
though either way the name means "camel handler"
and I prefer to think of Zoroaster
as an early version of St. Francis working
with people equally thick-skulled
to whom he said "friend, if you will refrain
from incessantly punching your cow
it may give more milk," or "honey,
if you want more eggs, stop
twirling your chickens by their tails,"
and since his wisdom was practical
as well as spiritual the Persians adopted
Zoroastrianism as the state religion and
the Sassanian dynasty put a fire altar
on the back of all its coins—
not that the Zoroastrians worshiped fire,
they just saw its purity as manifestation
of God, or Mazdah—and all their emperors,
whose names sound like Tolkien made them up,
Ardashir and Sapur and Yazdgard and Xusro,
ruled in the golden city of Zoroastrian light,
Ctesiphon, where flutes played erotic music
and the great merchants presided over banquets
where the most desirable women in the world
sang their learned poetry, their dear nipples rouged,
which now are dust, the emperors fled, vanished,
when the great horde of Allah,
the "horse people" Zoroaster feared who
need to subjugate and move on endlessly

burned the city with its famous towers
and blue fountains in the desert
all in the name of God

and only a few refugees reached India
where they became the Parsees of Bombay
who have "economic importance far greater
than their small numbers would indicate,"
and the encyclopedia names the great industrial
family of the Tatas—strange,
because the eldest Tata son, Ratan,
was my classmate at Cornell, he
with his soft eyes liquid as an animal's
who could assume the lotus position
and walk up stairs on his knees;
nor does the strangeness of their belief bother me:
Zoroaster's, that the world would endure just
12,000 years from the creation, or the Parsees'
exposure of their dead in "towers of silence"
for the vultures to devour, though we
know better, of course, and smile at anything,
for example the statue of the many-breasted Diana
at Ephesus, long ago destroyed by war, or the Manichees
who believed like Zoroaster that Satan was outside
the Power of God, and that the forces of the great light
and the great darkness were joined in equal battle,
and I believe, as did my catechizer, Pastor Hucke—
he who was so enthused playing
"A Mighty Fortress Is Our God"
that he once fell off his stool—
that it's heresy to believe wine is really turned to blood
though I remember the ladies of our church

dicing Wonder Bread into little cubes
("builds strong bodies eight ways")
to represent the Body of our Lord.

I'm sitting in an old farmhouse in the dark
late at night, and I too fear the horse people,
the President mad with good will and power,
old, blind and idiotic, who lines the missiles up.
Maybe because of Zoroaster
I scratch the bulldog's ears, and give him
a bit more of the liver and onions that he wants.
Bless the creatures. Bless us all in our absurdities.
I thank the distant and disinterested Ochester god
for Vivaldi, for physical love, for life, even
the loaf of Generic Wheat Bread my son has just devoured.
Given the small progress that we ever make I swear
I'll fix the chickens' leaking roof, and
I forgive the Pope his seven Rolls-Royces and
I'm happy that the Vatican is in the process
of forgiving Galileo for saying that the earth
revolves around the great fire after,
lord, only these 400 years.

THE MUSE

Quite a few of them, actually,
academic muses who are the sisters of Morpheus,
and the Medusa Muse who looks like *Il Duce*
and trades in various manifestations of hate, and
The New Yorker Muse, who is notoriously
dipsomaniacal and dances around on little
mouse feet, but my muse is a single mother
traveling north with a carful of kids,
she sends a postcard to say
"still feeling sorry for yourself?
still feeling paranoid?"
My muse was the first muse to hide
her stash behind a loose ceiling tile
in Ithaca, NY, and had the lowest recorded
average for a graduating senior, my muse
got married in the nude to a bartender
in the woods and regretted it shortly
afterward. My muse
knew Big Bill Haywood.
My muse has been keeping ten cats
in a small apartment and is slow
to change the litter. My muse
reads Brecht and sometimes pretends
she's Lotte Lenya; just when I think
she's settling down she shows up
with one immense Mona Lisa earring.
Once, on the rock hill in back of my house,
she said: "Look, give it up, all you know
is that if you're any good maybe you'll know more
tomorrow, and why shouldn't you wear
your heart on your sleeve, in your case
it needs fresh air, and as for form,
O'Hara was right, if you're buying jeans

you might as well get them tight
as possible you can kiss me now."

O muse, come back, I'm lonely and pedestrian,
I'm reading *USA Today*, and I'm afraid
and feel powerless and there's Reagan
and his undeclared wars

Ο ΠΡΟΚΤΟΣ
how many times
must I tell you
whatever blossoms
is rooted in the dark.

THE HEART OF OWL COUNTRY

Whatever blossoms is rooted
in the dark as, item

the delicate purple comfrey flower
supported by a brutish taproot

that powers itself into the subsoil
and splits the shale a dozen feet

beneath me, so that the bumblebees
tumble in a drunken frenzy here, and

item, how if I tend my loneliness,
which is no rarer than yours,

friend, I grow stronger,
so that my fists open, and the garden

becomes a natural metaphor for what
we have always known:

that only by going deeply
as possible into our dark

can we discover ourselves
to others, and even though

the stutterer I have always been
would like to say "we will never

die" I know that we will utterly
except for what we yield to friends

or progeny—that's the garden part—
and I remember now what I'd forgotten

for years, how, once, when we were
driving to my mother's, in New York State,

at twilight passing through a large marsh
my daughter said *look!* and in every dead

tree there was an owl, hundreds of them,
stupid in the light, like a faculty senate,

staring uncomprehendingly at the swamp
and the cars on the interstate, so still

one could have knocked them off their
perches with a stick and my daughter

screamed, delighted, "this must be
the heart of owl country!" and it

was: those soft fists of feathers
waiting for their hour, long

after we'd passed lifting into the spring air
on their solitary flights, each silent

in its large community, alert and perfect.

POEM ON HIS 44th BIRTHDAY

After so many years I've discovered
what my family taught me, they
who never saw gill-over-the-ground
or at least could not name it.
My mother must have been thinking of it
in the typing pool, saying to herself:
be like those cheerful leaves;
no matter how often you pull
or slash it the foot of its root
will venture out. In drought it
sends its small purple flowers up.
My uncle with his acid-stained hands
and eaten-out sweaters must have known
driving the battery truck:
wait long enough and the stripmine will flower,
the birds will return and dock plants will root,
the acid leach out of the ground
through the growing humus and grasses.

This must be why they kept flowers
in the gray house, and the dusty ivy
and indestructible snakeplants
which fried and seethed on the radiators.
Even my father, whose heart exploded
between two giant spruces he'd planted
with his pale hands years ago
must have known it, going down,
as he fell for the last time
to the earth and his fingers clawed in,
and the birds whose names he never knew
finally settled and continued
their only and endless song:
rejoice, rejoice.

ROCK HILL

Standing midway on the rock hill,
thinking of the sea, I want to gesticulate
and be theatrical, I want to shout
Thalassa, Thalassa to name her because
I remember how, years ago, we floated
like a pod of whales, massive and
oblivious, in the chop off Truro,
smoking cigars in the sea
as our friends watched and
neither the audacity of the waters
nor the idiocy of youth mattered
to what we were, white paddlers
asserting ourselves, drifting
into our futures with cigars
fuming like steamships.
                              But
here on the rock hill I want
more than my old story I want not just
gesture, but particular, not me but me
among the articulations of the creatures,
the hummingbird searching the beanflowers,
its iridescent breast big as a bumblebee,
this corn dropping pollen in sunlight
and moonlight, what I forget till I walk here,
the other dim lives suffering this world
and glorying in it, the intelligent
imprinted roots of the squash vines &
the vines sprawling through and around the corn,
the carrots with their sexual thrust
and stolidity.
                    A cat arches her back
in the sun and dares me to speak:

"A tiny beetle with six dots on its carapace
labors over a pebble, a green tomato worm
the size and shape of my thumb is going
deathward, its back bristling with white
parasite eggs." This poem is never going
to end, me here with my memories and this
fresh world, and the children distant in the house
their lovely youth making them immortal
as the sea slaps their bodies
and the sun sails by.

HAVING BUILT THE COOP

for centuries I have been forced
to sleepwalk on these roads of decay
—d.a.levy
The North American Book of the Dead

I put the chickens in and they swivel
their necks, tentative, suspicious,
their merciless unblinking eyes
reminders that they descended
from reptiles, though these are loveable
as they coo and cluck and their behinds
wiggle as they settle down to turn
the tiny compound into a mud flat
and then don't even try to escape,
though the grass they love is growing
luxuriantly a few inches beyond
the woven wire fence, because the coop
is home and from my point of view
I want their eggs in one basket
even though it's the nature of chickens
insofar as one can talk about "nature"
to be pecking through a broad universe
of an acre or more, and I suppose
the moral, if there is a "moral,"
is what levy said: it's all illusion,
but you may as well follow your own
as the illusions of others—though the chickens
don't care, the chickens cackle over some
culled spinach they adore and a handful
of cracked corn and cluck "this is
the best place in the world" though
of course they haven't been to any other
because they're in a cage but that's ok,

they don't live too long and they're
not likely to read Thucydides or
hit many good restaurants, they
are there to work, and it amazes me
how intelligent levy was for someone
who died at 23 but still understood
that "everyone pays their dues
& no one's getting the product"
though that was twenty years back
and none of the chickens are complaining
this June as the invisible cicadas sing
derrida • derrida • derrida

THANKSGIVING

On the tube, the old parade:
they've shoveled the shit off the streets
to make room for the starlets and
Conan the Barbarian with that tight helmet
to keep his skull screwed down and
His Eminence the Archbishop of NY
waves as though to say "howdy folks,
I hope you're not contemplating
an abortion" and the Arkansas Razorback
Marching Band plays some of Mozart's
greatest hits from *Amadeus* and the sun
blesses everything like a kid
watching tv with one eye
on his homework and

I see myself there in a brown snowsuit
with a zippered hood, waving
a diminutive flag above the crowd
and yelling to my father "higher!
hold me higher!" in front of an automat
where I learned later bums & kids went
for free lemonade, got lemon wedges
from the condiment trays and sugar
to mix with free ice at the water cooler—
one of the few mercies the city provided
but stopped giving long since—and
to which my father took me for years
for his favorite restaurant meal,
automat beans, baked in little brown pots
with a thin glaze of pork grease on top

and explained, always, that there was no
other city in the world where you could put
quarters and nickels in a slot and
get a pot of beans like that and

here's a band from Williamsport, PA—
"a town that's more than just Little League"
says Bobby Arnold the MC, who played
a corpse on *V*—doing its "unique" rendition
of "Stardust" beneath the world's first and largest
floating rubberized deconstructionist critic
masquerading as The Michelin Man and as far
as I can see this thing goes on forever,
dwarfs and Prince and minimum wage teens
carrying buckets and brooms behind
the Aleppo Shrine Horse Patrol and Placido Domingo
("hey man, don't step in the Placido Domingo!")

LOVE POEM WITH BOMB

Didn't Pius VIII say
"every new Christian brings us
a bit closer to Armageddon"?
Maybe we should all read Aristotle's
Rhetoric again, though it may
be too late in the day for that
since the barbarians are not
only at the gates but collecting
the tolls; hardly anyone knows
that Carlos Williams proposed
but O'Hara delivered, and let's face it:
if you concentrate your energies
on killing you don't have time
to learn why you shouldn't kill,
like the colonel in 'Nam who said
"the trouble with you guys is
you'd rather fuck than fight"
(wouldn't you?)

Nostradamus said: "Beware
the country that publishes
the most self-help books,"
but because I don't understand him
myself, I have to face the possibility
we'll survive; either way
I'll go down with you.
The giant oak I see from the bathroom
is slowly unfurling its leaves like
it means to hang around, and at night
the fat moths bounce off the glass.
For millennia we've been holding hands
in the dark again and again.

APRIL, NEAR THE SCHOOL FOR THE BLIND

I come up to
a column of blind children,
two by two, holding hands,
led by their teacher,
out for a walk in the sun
and four have fallen behind,
stalled at a garden where one
has picked a crocus and
is tearing at it with his teeth,
tasting crocus, delicately,
chewing and tasting, and
the teacher halts the group
and runs back to yell
what are you doing?
will you please
tell me what you're doing?

FOR THE MARGRAVE OF BRANDENBURG

When I'm driving up Bellefield in spring
with the window down and Bach needling
the air, Bach at the celestial sewing machine,
as the magnolia petals fall to the pavement
like fleshy coins, I think of you, and your daughters
if you had any—and you must have had them,
any uncle of the King of Prussia must have had
dozens of little dumplings dressed in silk,
and sons, all pimply in wigs, dabbling at harpsichords,
and not getting it right, poor things—
when the gift of the concerti first arrived
from Bach at Anhalt-Cothen, how your daughters
wrinkled their noses and puffed their waxed apple
cheeks, and the sons attended to their nose hairs
as the little clutch of journeymen musicians
you kept fiddled and squeaked, drops
of sweat plopping from their upper lips
as they labored over music too difficult to play
but which still said, plainly, O dumplings!
O zits! *macht auf* with the periwigs,
into the woods, the sunned air, the freshets
of vertiginous water, when you die you are dead
for so long no niceties of taffeta or toupee,
no good regard of the godful will redeem your death,
don't let my masses mislead you to studied solemnity,
serious doesn't mean solemn, necessarily, (signed:)
Papa Bach, Papa Bach, Papa Bach.

POEM FOR DR. SPOCK

I too when I die do not wish
to encumber my friends with the burdens
of sorrow: I want a simple ceremony,
twenty minutes or so, a few poems,
a brief testimonial, a tear or two
against plain black velvet and
as for the corpse burn it, scatter
the ashes around my asparagus plants,
which need large infusions of lime,
or throw them in the eyes of my enemies,
and let the mourners go off to a party,
a staid one where the waiters pour rivers
of Dom Perignon and nobody has to worry
about money for once, and later
a wild one with live music, a reappearance
of the Bonzo Dog Band, if possible, and
recapitulations of every drug popular
for the last fifty years, laughter
and solidarity for days. Let them stay
as long as they wish and then go
satiated, prepared again for the world,
and let the mouse of grief
gnaw at their hearts forever.

THE LAND OF COCKAIGNE

WHATEVER IT IS

I took some stones
from the overgrown fireplace
not too far from the maples
my father planted
that have outlived the house.
I have the tiny diamond
Aunt Barbara got from the man
she never spoke about
in my presence; today
only three people in the world
have any memory of her.
Here's a diary entry I made
as a teenager: "Cicero says
one of the 'six mistakes of man'
is to worry about things that
cannot be changed or corrected."

The stones are in the basement.
The diamond's in the vault.
Since I live in the country,
every spring I give a handful
of my hair clippings to the birds,
tie it in a bunch near a feeder
and let them pick at it to weave
into their nests, and perhaps into
their songs, these little
descendants of the dinosaurs who
sing and sing and we smile at them
because we think their song says
"nothing to worry about,
nothing to worry about."

OH BY THE WAY

My friend April Fallon tells me
that blood on the exterior of the brain
is cooler than that in the interior
and that it's in the cooler blood
that dreams reside.
What do you think?
Do you love the head as much as I do?
that calcareous shell, the stoniest part
of the body. And the stone
within the skull, the maker of imperatives,
of absolutes, that directed the trains
to the death camps. The brain
has no nerves to feel pain,
that stone that gave assent
to the show trials—that Stalinist part
of the body—and the saturation bombings,
Cambodia, Dresden, you name them.
What do you think?
The overexamined life isn't worth living.
That veil of cool blood
where dreams reside; there even now
an old scholar rests his eyes
behind his hands; the farmer exerts
the requisite pressure on the cow's teats
for milk, in that pastoral memory;
the old woman wracked by pertussis
will be saved from her poverty.
Thin cool veil of blood.
What do you think?
I have to stop writing about love.
I have to stop making sense.

Cool veil of blood, old dreams:
Jeffords pushed against the bronze
school doors, red stain on white shirt,
kid with the knife:
"motherfuckin motherfucker"
(deconstruct that);
the child whispering "Help me help me."
O thin veil of blood
where dreams reside
cool veil of blood.

READING JOYCE

I don't know how I learned about *The Portrait*, or why
I had a copy of the Viking paper edition when I was 12
and took it into the hay and goldenrod on the hill
to read it. Do you remember how golden the light
is in August when you're 12? How anything
might happen? How the Prince of the Air
or any other miracle you'd read in a book
might come down to you and lift you up?
I couldn't understand Joyce. Above me
a chicken hawk was circling, and I lay back,
watching it float so easily. Already my father
was on the road to the distant place from which
he never returned. His brothers were in the house
talking big about the money that never showed.
I guess I believed in them. I guess if you'd asked me
I'd have said they were fine people. I guess
if you'd asked me I'd have said it was fine
that my mother had turned her back to get
the bob and the perm, and that all I knew
from the women in the kitchen were the clacking
of pots and the clucking. I didn't know
a damn thing, except that when I saw
the snapping turtle, I put my book down.
It was big as a plate, and nasty, with spines
on its back and claws that hollowed out
a hole two feet wide and deep. I offered
a stick, which it snapped in half. I didn't know
shit. I thought my father would come back.
I thought my mother loved me. The turtle
was laying eggs, eggs, eggs, it kept its eye
on me and the eggs kept popping out.

When I called, no one came. If I'd touched
the turtle, I would have lost a finger.
Everyone but me knew what they were doing.
Well, I was pretty young.
Joyce came later.

THE BARN

The bat lay grinning on the stone
where we had shot it, its mouth
open and fanged, its eyes closed.

You could walk through the sweet timothy
in the loft, and fall through a rotten board.

Calvin had asked one of the Dalton sisters,
who was six or so, into the hay bales near
the broken tractor to play doctor, coaxing
her I think with candy or fruit. I was 10.
He was 10. We often played doctor
with one another. The Dalton girl wore
a white blouse and white pants. Before
anything happened, she started to cry
and I left, not the first time I'd
walked away. I walked up and down
the dirt road with its summer oil slick,
I walked back but was afraid to go inside.
I walked around the apple tree where
my other friend Walter had fallen off a branch
and had splintered his left arm and his
father had beaten him for it. I walked
back just as they were coming out of the dark
of the barn's mouth, into sunlight.
His hands had covered the crotch
of her white pants with grime, and
she was crying softly and walked away.

I walked to my place. I had the job
of picking blackberries, and I did that.
I was crying, and the berries set their
purple stain in my fingers. I waited
for a siren to cut the air, for the police
to come howling after me, but nothing
stirred. The sky was glass blue. A crow cawed
as they do, late in the summer.

DREAMING ABOUT MY FATHER

We're painting the old house in the Hudson Valley
and we're a team, applying the paint so smoothly
that not a drop gets spilled, it's all cream, and
for the first time he has no complaints about
the way I work. "Good job" he says and smiles
when we climb down the ladders and take a break
for a beer. He tells me again about how he loves
this place, how he loves the country, how poor
his family was, growing up in Brooklyn—how ashamed
he was that my grandmother had to take in washing
and scrubbed steps to meet the rent on their
smelly apartment on Chauncy Street—and for once
I listen to him without yawning. "Why don't we
pick some stones out of the garden?" he says,
and we do that, we take the old wheelbarrow
which doubles as a cement trough and pick
a couple of loads of stone from the rocky patch
where he grows golden bantam corn—his favorite—
and the beans, and the carrots that never form straight
roots, and the tomatoes in such abundance that
I still have photos of them, my grandmother smiling
over the bushels of red fruit in front of her.
The first hummingbird I ever saw as a child keeps
buzzing between the salvia and the rose of Sharon.
"I'm sorry," he says as we roll a load of stones
toward the wall he's building near the big maple,
"that I didn't talk to you more—what can I say?
I was tired and angry—and that I called you
good-for-nothing." "It's ok," I say, "that's
so long ago. I want you to know that after
you died I came back, after the airport expanded

and they took all the places on this road,
I came back twice. By the first time they'd
flattened everything, but I took a few stones
that were left from the fireplace you built
and I have them still." "That fireplace" he says,
"I taught myself how to build from stone."
I say: "Last year was the second time, it was
so grown over it was hard to find the place,
but I finally did because the red maples
you planted were still there among the wild trees."
"It's a shame" he says, "how they took the place
and never even used it, after all that work."
"Yes, but the catalpa trees you planted? they've
spread everywhere, it must be a half mile
in every direction, down to the brook and
up the hill near where the Dolans lived."
"I know," he says, "but it doesn't matter
now that we're here, and we're talking,
now that we don't even have to talk."

OCT. 27, 1989

And what did you want?
To call myself beloved, to feel myself
beloved on the earth.
    —*Ray Carver*

He was in a hotel in Baltimore
in a suburb near Johns Hopkins. He would

give a talk there, and they would pay him for it.
It was night, and he was alone; sirens were racing

up and down the streets. The room was very large.
Most of what he had wished for as a boy was to write poems,

to have some power with the word, to be paid
for talking. Don't smile, please. He wanted

to be put in a beautiful room like this.
Bonnie would pick him up in an hour. He saw

out the picture window a few men in trenchcoats
walking toward the parking lot, and beyond that

headlights and taillights on a freeway a mile
or so away. He'd been reading Carver's last book

of poems, reading "Gravy" and other valedictories.
He remembered Carver a few years before his death,

kidding about his prosperity, kneeling before his Mercedes
and waving a fistful of dollars, because he was so amazed,

he supposed, to have them, that good man, whose last poems,
written in the knowledge of imminent death, said

love the world, don't grieve overmuch, listen to people.
The beautiful room was a good place to read; he'd finished

the book (for the second time) at the pine desk, where
the indirect white light hurt his eyes. He didn't think

he'd ever be as famous as Carver, but who could tell?
He was sorry the man was dead; there was nothing

he could do about that, but he was sorry for it.
He got up to look out the picture window. He could

see the red spintops of some cops' cars. Other than that
nothing special: in the entrance courtyard a lone cabbie

smoked a cigarette; spotlights shone up through the yellow
foliage of a clump of maples. A few slow crickets.

He had everything he really wanted, he had learned
that friends, like love, couldn't save him.

THE DRY TORTUGAS

The seaplane lifts off in a surge of spray
like a heavy duck, and the gentleman in suspenders
yells "ee-YOW" in triumph, and we're all together now,
the old radical from Wisconsin in the blue Lenin cap
and Windjammer t-shirt, the spruce Navy commander,
the co-pilot who rests her hand on the pilot's knee,
the guy with the potbelly and Robert Bly smile
who is greenly airsick after takeoff,
the sixtyish debutante in the linen skirt,
the beautiful woman who, though told not to,
will hide a piece of fan coral in her backpack—
wherever we have come from, whatever bad deals
we have done, whatever sadnesses or lost dreams,
we are free of the continent at last, we are looking
for the dugong and manta in the shallow waters,
we are passing over the wreck of "The Princess"
demolished by naval gunners for practice, we
are passing over the wreck of "The Republic," and
we are flying over the atolls of the Marquesas
(the co-pilot pronounces it "at-holes" and says
"an at-hole is a lagoon surrounded by coral reef,
and in the Marquesas we have the largest at-hole
in the United States," and someone cheers)
and then we set down in the Tortugas next to
Bush Island, knee-deep in guano from the nesting
sooty terns and noddy terns and the frigate birds
gliding overhead, and we are one with the laughing gulls
and the common loon, the northern parulas and
the black skimmers and the Bonaparte's gull,
so that whatever nastiness was in us is purged
by the limpid brine and the gentle surf,

and we are all pickled in it now, all
smiling, all bobbing like coconuts
floating off to start a new world, and Lenin,
grizzled and scarred, battle-worn and lost,
is singing off-key and mugging and
we all laugh with him, memory lost
as we dogpaddle in the sea.
We have given ourselves up
to the baptism of pleasure.
We are reborn.
We will never do evil again.

COOKING IN KEY WEST

Start with Key West golden shrimp
("the color of the gold they found
in the sunken treasure ships" the woman
behind the counter says, and smiles,
lifting her eyes to heaven) and then
some finocchio from the Waterfront Market
and some lime juice, a salad of radicchio
and watercress, and a bottle of Pescevino—
"fish wine"—in the fish-shaped bottle;
"I wonder what the poor people are doing"
my father would have said, and I don't know,
not too many of them at Fort Zach Taylor beach
this morning, a Cuban family lugging deck chairs
rented at $6/per, and a lot of college kids,
a middle-aged dyke couple going in and
out of the water every few minutes, and some
gay guys walking up and down the strand,
remarkably tanned and fit, even though
the gay culture in Key West has been
pretty well decimated by AIDS and I'm
stirring wine into the shrimp and think of
Donnie, the kid buried in the family plot
in Grafton, MA, in an unmarked grave because
he died of AIDS and hadn't, of course,
turned out the way his family wanted,
so they put him in the poverty
of an unmarked grave, *sans* shrimp,
sans radicchio, *sans* everything and
of course I'm crying like a fool by now,
honking into my red pocket bandana

and pouring more wine, thinking of the family
that hated their son so much that they lowered
his poor body into such a grave.

I don't know anything.
I'm just learning how to see and to hear.
I want to find a way to say and believe: live,
don't be afraid until you have to be.
When you're dead you'll forget everything.
Not far from here Hemingway
had a character say: "To me
the visible world is visible."

FOR MY SON NED

—who complained, humorously, that I've written
more poems about his sister than about him

Tip O'Neill said, after Kennedy was shot,
"there's no sense in being Irish if you don't know
the world will break your heart" but since
I'm mainly Polish I'm not sure the latter part
of that is true, and in any event I want to say
don't trust in gab too much. It's like
in a bowling game at a bar, you can put
sawdust all over the table of the machine
and maybe you'll get a strike and you call that
skill, but when you get a split or worse
you say "bad luck," but what the hell, you'll
have another beer. Poems are like that,
and since this is the only advice I've ever
given you in a poem, I'd be remiss not
to point out certain similarities to "Life."

And I also want to say that when you were born
the nurse said, humorously I think,
"my God, look at that" and pointed
to your hair standing on end as though
just born you knew what lay ahead,
and I won't dwell on the times
I stayed up half the night
worrying about you & this & that, all
pointless worries of course lost
in the ancient photo album of my brain.
Marx said "freedom is the recognition
of necessity," and he might have been

speaking of the little that we know
of the obscure impulse we call love. And
in any event we're stuck with one another and
of course no one can ever be praised too much.
So I'm lifting a beer in your direction and
I want to say thirty-some years after
the momentous event of your birth: "hello?"
and, "I'm trying to redress the balance"
and, "welcome to the world."

AT THE POETRY READING

in the library I am very decorous and read
what I think are my quietest poems, and
my least nasty, except for the two
about Pocahontas being a sexually active
twelve year old and the one about Jesus
as a parasitic insect, and all-in-all
I am a good deal less shocking than
a Quentin Tarantino movie or, for that matter,
Men in Black, and a few younger students yawn
as if to underline the fact, but I see Ann,
my student from the "College for the Over Sixty"
and what seems to be an elderly friend of hers
and afterward they come up to me holding
hands: Ann is nervous and may
be blushing, though she says it's so good
to hear my new poems, but her friend appears
to be in a state of shock, and mutters:
"it's another world, another world,"
and I almost lie "it's not my fault! I don't
want to make you unhappy! I just write
what I see!" as they backpedal and say
"goodbye, goodbye nice to meet you" and
totter off to the real world: Ronald McDonald,
The Phantom of the Opera, Christmas clubs,
Princess Diana, Oprah on a diet, the statue
of the Virgin Mary weeping in the North Hills. . . .

MY FIRST BRASSIERE

> And then I looked into the mirror on my
> dresser, beside us . . . and there we were:
> Betty June's face buried in the pillow; me
> gangly as a whippet and braying like an ass. It
> was marvelously funny; I exploded with laughter.
> —*John Barth, The Floating Opera*

My friend Judith is asking her class to write poems
titled "My First Brassiere" (or "Condom") and says
that she'll write a poem herself on the subject though
"I'm not going to write a poem praising brassieres,
and I'm not going to write one about being a *persona*
of brassieres, because I wasn't one, and I'm not
going to be a fetishist like Marianne Moore wearing
a three-cornered brassiere because that's just too
obscure; I mean, I just wear brassieres," but as she
speaks I think of my own nervousness with such things,
not brassieres, particularly, but how the rocking motion
of the Myrtle Avenue bus as I stood and bounced to school
left me in a state of such excitation that I worried
IT would be perceptible to some sweet ancient
sitting 6" from my crotch; and before that, how
doing jumping jacks in sixth grade gym led
to such enormous (I thought) erections that I was led
to try strapping the offending member to my leg
with rubber bands—and didn't that smart, with all
the little red rings around it like the tail
of a bald and embarrassed raccoon; and later
in college once an ill-advised move I made caused
a condom to fly off me like an exhausted birthday
balloon, so that it flew through the room
with the erratic motion natural to deflating
latex projectiles and actually stuck
to the wall; and after that, when I imagined
I had learned as much as there was to know about sex,

I had to find excuses when Ellen at 4:00 pm ran up
the stairs wearing only an old raccoon coat and a pair
of sneakers, because I was probably an idiot but I was
writing my honors thesis on Wallace Stevens and didn't
wish to be disturbed.
                    I'm sorry for nothing, and
I've learned so much from my mistakes that I could
repeat each one with pleasure, and I'd also say
that sex has taught me two things:

don't judge
but if you must judge,
forgive.

ON FRANK O'HARA'S BIRTHDAY, KEY WEST

The woman behind me at the Half Shell Bar
says "there are two anagrams for the word fear:
'fuck everything and run' and
'face everything and recover' and
I'm trying to do the latter"

and since it's the same with me
after my stupid heart failed and
I was life-flighted, etc. etc.,
I have to applaud the intention,

but I'm in my usual Key West glow
and loving the silliness, the tourists
at Hemingway's house photographing
the descendants of his cats.
Whenever I float in the chop
off Fort Taylor I think maybe
I'm among H2O molecules Hemingway
or Elizabeth Bishop touched here
or O'Hara waded through off Fire Island,
perhaps not.

Where do the polished glass pebbles
on the beach come from?—lovers
long ago who smashed the bottles
on the rocks or secret drinkers
in despair? All of them say
"remember me, remember me,"
but today the huge Cuban families
come to sing and to picnic
and boom-box salsa drives the ghosts away.

I'm glad Hemingway punched Wallace Stevens
here, thus minimizing the idea of order
at Key West, and God bless the tourists
walking up and down Duval,
all they want is pleasure and some memories,
all they want is permanence and
they won't find it, though luckily
when the sun sets behind the La Concha
and the tourists applaud it and
lift their glasses in toast
the sun will come back again. In ten years
it'll be the same but they won't.

If I could comfort anyone I would
but the best I can do is remember
a sentiment of my semi-literate grandma,
who knew almost nothing beyond
cooking ("what a potato salad!") and being kind.
She said "if you remember someone you love
and you really care for them
they can never really die."

Well, she was wrong.
But because she really cared for me
she would always ask: "Are you happy?"
And I would always have to say
"Yes, I am happy. Yes, I am."

WHAT THE FROST CASTS UP

A crown of handmade nails, as though
there were a house here once, burned,
where we've gardened for fifteen years;
the ceramic top of an ancient fuse;
this spring the tiny head of a plastic doll—
not much compared to what they find
in England, where every now and then
a coin of the Roman emperors, Severus
or Constantius, works its way up, but
something, as though nothing we've
ever touched wants to stay in the earth,
the patient artifacts waiting, having been lost
or cast away, as though they couldn't bear
the parting, or because they are the only
messengers from lives that were important once,
waiting for the power of the frost
to move them to the mercy of our hands.

CHICKADEE

Late at night when the house is silent
I'll put down my book and quarter an apple
or put a few slivers of cheese on a piece
of flatbread, and it must be the poverty
of those meals which makes me think
of the departed, like the old German
who used to walk hunched every afternoon
past my window when I was very small
and wave to me, his walrus moustache
yellowed by cigars (back then all the old
men smoked and they lived forever)
which he held in an amber mouthpiece.
No one in my house knew him, but he waved
just the same, and tapped his cane toward
the corner where the cop stood directing
traffic, but stopped long enough to
tip his cap to the old man, as though
it were a Bing Crosby movie and not
a lousy corner in Queens on an eight-lane
boulevard. And I think again of Fat Charley,
his huge head—thin black hair parted down
the middle—floating above his beer stein,
and his terrible jokes—every 4th of July:
"the blessings of liberty for ourselves
and our posteriors"—and again of my father
walking dark tenement streets in Brooklyn,
collecting crumpled bills from the poor
for their small policies, life & casualty.

I'm sick of pity because it's pointless,
almost always self-referential. This morning,
this warm day in March 500 miles from that

corner in the city, I listened to the birds
in the hawthorn—such singing, and snow is
expected—such difficult lives. One chickadee
came close to inspect me, hopping from
branch to branch to get a better view, until
I could see her carpet-tack beak as she
studied me, cool and fearless, this creature
that weighs an ounce, with her merciless
black-bead reptilian eye.

IN PRAISE OF WILLIAM STAFFORD

He had one of those faces
I can't remember exactly
it was so plain—
as a wheatfield is plain,
as a lake in sunlight—
and many of his poems
are like that.
They remind me of things
that sometimes I'd rather
forget: the day
I promised myself
I would never be cruel
to anyone, the day
a goldfinch in its elliptical
flight was the most beautiful
thing I'd ever seen. I was young
and usually one keeps such things
hidden. You know how it is.

But sometimes
when the world recedes
it comes back to you,
like that loose strand
of spider web you feel sometimes
in a summer hammock—
momentarily puzzling,
nearly invisible but
connected to something.

POCAHONTAS

Disney didn't tell you
that when she first
slept with Captain Smith
she was 12 years old and
at that time
organized nude dancing
by her young friends
for the delectation of the colonists.
If this disturbs you deeply
you're probably beyond help.
You should go to Orlando
and stand in line for three hours in the rain.
Take a snapshot of Goofy.

Oh, two other things: in colonial
Virginia the age of sexual consent
was 10. And, if you eat
of the fruit of Disney
you will die.

THE NIGHT OF THE LIVING DEAD

Like a parasitic insect, stealthy Jesus
lays his eggs at the base of their skulls
and they hatch, raven through
the medulla, cerebellum and
the cerebrum: they are "saved,"
they are "blissful," they are
"born again." They wear galoshes,
they have sex only for procreation,
they are unemployed, they are
bound for glory because
they know one thing
(the only thing to know)
and they want to give it to you.
They are gathered this evening
before your door to offer tracts,
they are restrained, they don't
like to touch themselves, they
are standing here today quietly
though they burned Jews, though they
stoned heretics, though they inserted
flaming pokers into the anuses
of homosexuals. They're restrained, they
know God, they would like to tear
your arms from your sockets, they
are waiting until the world is dark enough
to tear the flesh from your thighs.

WHAT HE DID IN BIRMINGHAM IN APRIL

—for Mike Srba

I cried a lot, what with the news
of Mike's lymphoma, and all the poems
I was rereading bubbling as though
from memory through my lips,
and I saw from a new angle how poems
transmute pain. I spent hours talking
to my students. "Art can erase grief
through the force of the creative mind"
Amy Shields wrote, so serious I told her
it was ok to laugh at a funny poem.
I laughed a lot. I usually do;
I don't want to mislead you.
I listened to music. I got up early
and cooked grits nearly every morning,
and I became tidy, scrubbed the dishes
every noon, careful not to break
the delicate yellow ceramic bowl
from Paris (this is just a real bowl,
dear Amy, it doesn't stand for anything)
and I reread Cavafy and *To Have and Have Not*
and was careful to water the basil plants
and rosemary Mike & Betsy got me for a gift,
and when a poem came by I tried to write it.
I tried not to make anything up.
I took an elevator to the top of Vulcan,
"the world's largest cast iron statue."
I tried not to explain too much to myself.
I edited some mss., I edited Natasha Saje's
beautiful book with the poems about food and
the one called "A Short History of the Sybarites"
and I drove around Birmingham in the rain.
I laughed a lot, to tell the truth, and

I was always on the phone. I tried some wines
I hadn't tried before, vernaccia and
Chateau de Cabriac and some pretty good merlots.
I drove around Birmingham in the rain.

THE WREN AND HIS CHILDREN

Every morning when I sit on my porch
the wren balances on his house upside down
or sits on his favorite black walnut twig
and sings to me. His song is at least
three times as big as his body. He's happy
to have carried moths to his brood,
their open red mouths at the entrance hole.
What he likes best, or they do,
are white moths the size of a quarter,
and he comes back every thirty seconds
or so with another (I've timed it),
as though he were piecing together
tiny bits of linen for a quilt, or
were an historian collecting precious
scraps of an ancient manuscript.
And then he sings, loudly:
"bubbling, exuberant" is how
the *Field Guide* describes it.
He seems to like the work for its own sake—
he never stops to gaze fondly at his children—
and in spring he or his offspring busily
dismantle an old nest twig by twig
and then use the old twigs to put
the nest back together again.

After a day's work, when I sit on the porch
and smoke my cigar, the wren sings to me
as though giving an account of *his* day,
and once again I admire the animals,
how they never question their motives
and rarely doubt themselves.
How happy he is, or
if it isn't happiness,
what is it?

FOR GANESHA, HINDU GOD OF GOOD FORTUNE

—and for Gerald Stern

In a week I'll be leaving
the only place I've ever been happy
living alone, I'll leave the red hills
of Birmingham and my monastic life where
I've written poems in silence and reread
Richard Farina and some other books
we used to live by, and every morning
washed the blue salt-glaze Japanese bowls
I've eaten my rice and grits from,
and I'll be leaving you, Ganesha, with your
broken tusk in your right hand and
the sweet rice cake (your favorite food)
in your left, as I drive due north
away from the Museum of Art, and
I'll think of you, god of wisdom
and good fortune, so much like my own
clumsy life and good luck lately.
The ancients report that you were
decapitated "in an unfortunate accident,"
that the gods gave you an elephant's head.
They said that you broke off your left tusk
to write the sacred books for the gods,
and you sit tonight in the dark Museum
with a self-satisfied grin, and the tusk
in your right hand and sweet rice cake
in your left, having done what you could
in improbable circumstances, as I sit
on my porch with a glass of semillon and
a bowl of rice, watching the clouds
and the moon rising, and I will remember you

when I pray for the ones I love,
elephant face, grotesque and serene, and
when I leave here on the interstate
worrying my loose tooth, speeding away
from the barbecue at Dreamland,
and the blue tiled pools in the garden, and
the rough cabin where Ted sang Puccini to himself
because he was so happy cooking steaks while
I sat drinking wine on the deck, and away
from the carp pool in the Birmingham
Japanese garden where the fat man
with a camera asked me to photograph
himself and his friend—his charge—the kid
with palsy, whose head lolled from side to side
as they stood on the bridge and waved above the water,
while the carp, the koi, swam in schools around
around and around the little pond.

Oh Ganesha, I know happiness is fragile, I know
we disappear like the mallow flowers by the roadside
in spring, I know how clumsy we are,
but I'll think of you as I leave, driving home
as the insane Alabama drivers going 90
flip me a finger as they pass and
I'll flip one back because I'm glad
to have been in my silence, and now to leave it,
oh cripple and fool and holy one.

DESIGN AND PRODUCTION

Text and cover design by Kathy Boykowycz.

Text set in Stone Serif, designed in 1987 by Sumner Stone.
Titles set in Futura Bold Condensed, based on the Futura font
designed in 1928 by Paul Renner, Germany.

Printed by Thomson-Shore of Dexter, Michigan,
on Nature's Natural, a 50% recycled paper.